Physical Education
FOR
ELEMENTARY SCHOOLS

III

19747

PHYSICAL EDUCATION FOR ELEMENTARY SCHOOLS

Library of Congress Catalog Card Number 57–11851

Physical Education
for Elementary Schools

McGraw-Hill Series in Health Education, Physical Education, and Recreation

CLIFFORD LEE BROWNELL, *Consulting Editor*

RUTH EVANS

*Director of
Physical Education for Women
Springfield College
Springfield, Massachusetts*

THELMA I. BACON

*Elementary School Teacher
Springfield, Massachusetts*

MARY E. BACON

*Elementary School Principal
Springfield, Massachusetts*

JOIE L. STAPLETON

*Chairman,
Women's Physical Education
University of Kansas
Lawrence, Kansas*

1958

McGraw-Hill Book Company, Inc.

NEW YORK   TORONTO   LONDON

Consulting Editor's Preface

The authors of *Physical Education for Elementary Schools* bring to their subject a wealth of professional preparation which has been tested in the laboratory of practical experience. Sound professional preparation gives insight into such intricate matters as the psychology of learning, child growth and development, appropriate subject-matter experiences, various methodologies, educational administration and consultant services, and total evaluation. Practical experience fuses these disciplines into a composite and unified whole as educators deal effectively with individual children, a class, the entire school, and the community at large.

The authors represent a variety of professional backgrounds that relate to the conduct of physical education in elementary schools. In the first place, two of them attained marked success as classroom teachers—a position in which Thelma Bacon continues to serve with distinction. Mary Bacon is a superior elementary-school principal who properly regards her primary function as curriculum development for wholesome community education. For several years Ruth Evans gained prominence as a supervisor or consultant in physical education for the Springfield, Massachusetts, public schools, before joining the teacher-education staff at Springfield College. Joie Stapleton has had thorough and sound experience in the major department of physical education at the University of Kansas. This combination in authorship facilitates the application of contemporary educational theory tempered by the exigencies of everyday practice.

Perhaps two special features characterize the excellence of this text: first, the outstanding program of physical education developed in the elementary schools of Springfield during the past quarter-century, and, second, the combined efforts of the authors, whose shared experiences helped markedly to achieve the distinction in physical education which Springfield now enjoys. Thus all the materials contained in this volume have been tested for their validity by practical and efficient educators working with real children under actual school conditions in a cosmopolitan community and in a laboratory school.

CLIFFORD L. BROWNELL

Preface

The depth and scope of experiences and activities in elementary schools continually increase. All these experiences and activities influence elementary education. Through a careful blending of learnings, which is the result of daily experiences and activities, children develop those qualities which open doors that lead to opportunity for successful and rich living in a modern society. It is the responsibility of elementary schools to provide an atmosphere that builds a foundation for effective citizenry.

Physical education provides many widely varied opportunities for experiences which contribute to the enrichment of personal well-being and social adjustment. This book discusses many of these opportunities and explains how a well-planned program of physical education may become an essential part of the total school program, how physical education serves as an indicator of physical fitness, and how such fitness contributes to the total welfare of children.

In planning and organizing the book, the authors have endeavored to fulfill a threefold purpose:

1. To present a guide for use by classroom teachers in planning and presenting their programs of physical education
2. To provide a textbook for use by classroom teachers in their pre- or in-service professional preparation
3. To clarify for the specialist in physical education general problems faced by classroom teachers

Classroom teachers will find suggested methods for applying the principles involved in the unit approach to physical education. They will also find resources and ideas for daily lesson plans. The book explains the advantages of both long-term planning and immediate or short-term planning. It outlines planned programs that ensure a balance among the various types of physical activity, and it describes and presents directions for conducting rhythmic activities, self-testing activities, and play activities.

For prospective teachers of physical education in elementary schools, the book provides a background for developing desirable attitudes toward education in general and physical education in particular. It states a philosophy of elementary education and explains how physical education contributes to the fulfillment of this philosophy. To support its theoretical contentions, the book delineates the methods and materials of the physical education program and offers suggestions for successful integration of subject matter. Describing the characteristics of different age groups of elementary-school children, it explains basic teaching methods applicable to all age groups and recommends procedures for use with each age group. Similarly, it describes the environment conducive to satisfactory progress for children at each age level and for individuals within each age group.

For the specialist in physical education, this book describes situations that facilitate a genuine understanding of teacher problems not always evident to the supervisor or consultant. It cites examples of teacher-supervisor cooperation which serve as a guide to the establishment of sound professional rapport. Persons using this book as a text for pre- or in-service education may prefer to study the material by sections rather than by chapters. Such a procedure enables the group to deal with larger bodies of related subject matter. The Questions and Problems for Discussion and Selected References arranged for each section may be used to advantage with this procedure.

RUTH EVANS

THELMA I. BACON

MARY E. BACON

JOIE L. STAPLETON

Acknowledgments

The authors wish to acknowledge, with gratitude and sincere appreciation, the interest manifested by:

Dr. Clifford Brownell for his inspirational guidance and helpful suggestions.

The administrators of the Springfield School System—Dr. T. Joseph McCook, Miss Alice Beal, and Mr. M. Marcus Kiley—from whom permission was obtained to take pictures of physical education activities in the elementary schools.

Miss Alice Conley and Miss Helen O'Connell, principals of the elementary schools where the pictures were taken.

Mr. Robert Berry and Miss Anna Marie Anderson of the Physical Education Department of the Springfield schools, for their approval of the pictures.

Miss Flora Bacon, Miss Barbara Hurley, Miss Jane Londergan, Mr. William O'Malley, Miss Margaret Ryan, and Miss Jane Worcester—teachers whose efforts and cooperation made the pictures possible.

Mrs. Mary Darling of The Darling Studio of Longmeadow, for her patience and generosity of time in photographing the activities.

Mrs. Alyce Bacon and Miss Judith McMullen for their assistance with the drawings and diagrams.

Mrs. Mabel Swanson for her assistance in typing the manuscript.

Houghton Mifflin Co. for permission to quote from "The Village Blacksmith."

The many administrators, teachers, children, and other school personnel with whom the authors have worked through the years, and from whom they have received inspiration and cooperation which have contributed to the writing of this book.

Contents

Part One

Planning the Program

1. The Open Door

The Nature of Elementary Education. Education is the sum of one's experiences during life's journey. Just so, elementary education is the sum of a child's experiences during his journey through the elementary grades. The nature of elementary education, therefore, depends upon the number and kinds of experiences a child has while he is enrolled in the elementary school. It is the teacher's responsibility to provide experiences sufficiently worthwhile to meet the needs of the elementary-school child. The following situations are presented as examples of the types of experiences often provided for children in elementary schools.

LEARNING THROUGH COOPERATIVE EXPERIENCES

One cloudy, foreboding April morning the fifth-grade children in Room 10 of Hamilton School rushed into the room all talking at once. They crowded around their teacher, Miss Brown, and led her to the work alcove in double-quick time. They pointed to the sky, which *did* look ominous. Their exclamations went something like this:

"Look, Miss Brown! What's that? Is it a planet? Will it bump us? We're scared!"

Miss Brown looked. There *was* something peculiar in the atmosphere. It seemed like hurricane weather but it wasn't the hurricane season. She could not explain it and she was not ashamed to say so. However, she recognized the opportunity to direct the children's thinking in a way that would allay their fears and, at the same time, help them to reach a satisfactory conclusion.

Cooperative Thinking. After the children had asked their questions and acknowledged their fears, they waited expectantly for Miss Brown's answers. She observed the sky for several seconds and then turned to face her pupils.

4

"It does look unusual up there," she said, "but *I'm* not afraid. Let's talk about it. Why do you think it is a planet, and what planet do you think it is?"

Ginny answered, "I think it's Mercury because it spins and moves along at the same time."

But Jack argued, "Oh no! It *doesn't* move. It just looks like it's moving. I think it's the sun behind the moving clouds."

"I think it's a phenomenon," put in Carolyn.

One child after another made comments concerning the "phenomenon," as many liked to call it. They substantiated their comments with sound, common-sense explanations. They used as a reference the bulletin board they had prepared following a recent class visit to the local planetarium. That visit to the planetarium and the bulletin board itself no doubt enhanced their interest in what they believed to be a phenomenon.

As the children stated many interesting and pertinent facts, their tension seemed to disappear. They forgot that they were frightened as they went from bulletin board to geography book to the window to compare what they had learned with what they saw.

Finally Miss Brown said, "If we are really viewing a phenomenon, where can we get immediate information about it?"

"I know," said Richard, the little professor of the class. "The radio will tell us." Richard went at once to the radio and tuned in the local station.

No information was forthcoming, but as they listened, glorious sunlight flooded the room and thirty-nine faces lighted up with happiness and relief. Their eyes spoke for them: "God's in *His* Heaven. All's right with the world." The children then proceeded with the business and pleasure of the day.

Controlled Informality. Every day in Room 10 does not begin with an incident as exciting and breathtaking as the one just described, but every day does present equally informal situations. Group discussions form an important part of the "before school" routine. In some of these discussions Miss Brown is invited to participate. If a discussion becomes too vociferous Miss Brown invites herself to take part, and the children's voices become calmer as she guides the discussion to a satisfactory conclusion. Some children gather to help one another with school problems or with problems encountered at a scout meeting. Informality is the keynote, and self-imposed order usually prevails.

Self-reliance. On Tuesdays the school "savers" meet in one corner of the room. They manage their own banking, entering their deposits and computing the totals in their bankbooks. Weekly tellers are appointed to prepare for the downtown bank the record sheet with the list of depositors, the total class deposits, and the percentage of the class participating. They plan campaigns to increase the number of class savers. The skill these pupils acquire as they assume responsibility for the entire process of their weekly banking program helps to develop a self-reliance which, under sound guidance, becomes useful to them in their study habits.

Self-direction. On Fridays this fifth-grade class collects the milk orders for the entire building. With guidance from the teacher, the children list the qualifications needed by those who might serve as collectors, recorders, money counters, and clerks. They classify themselves according to their own evaluations of the fitness needed for these various positions. Before the year ends, every child will have assisted in at least one step of the process and many children will have served in every step. The work becomes so organized that children can complete the entire job with little or no supervision by the teacher. They direct and check themselves through each step.

Development of Democratic Principles. Democracy operates in this classroom every day. It does not just happen; it results from continuous and conscious effort on the part of the teacher to help children develop those habits of self-discipline and self-direction that lead to many happy human relationships.

But do the democratic principles operate successfully only in the informal type of classroom situation? Not at all! In the same Hamilton School the children of another classroom work and play together in a truly democratic way but under more formal conditions.

Cooperative Formality. When the school bell rings in the morning the children of Room 14 enter the classroom, greet their teacher, and go at once to their assigned places. They know there is work to do before the regular school session begins and they do this work without question. When the session begins they participate in the opening exercises, which include scripture reading, a prayer, and the salute to the flag. Then the children and teacher share experiences of interest to all.

Mrs. White, the teacher of this classroom, works as conscientiously as Miss Brown to help her pupils develop habits of self-discipline, self-direction, and cooperation, but in a totally different way. Mrs. White's pupils enjoy many opportunities to become good leaders and good followers. They, as well as Miss Brown's pupils, recognize and appreciate their own special abilities and those of their classmates. All the children, therefore, contribute valuably to the school program.

Sharing Information. In this second classroom, children record the length of each day, the phases of the moon, and other information pertinent to the wonders of nature. They keep individual and class notebooks of these materials and prepare bulletin board notices that are used as references by children in other classrooms.

Developing Leadership. In Room 14 pupil leaders entertain groups of children by reading to them during reading parties. Mrs. White assigns children of different reading-ability levels as leaders of these groups. Although the activities of Mrs. White's pupils follow a more formal pattern than do those of Miss Brown's class, the former have equally challenging incentives and equally valuable results.

Democratic Living. Through experiences which develop good leaders and good followers, children of these classrooms have opportunities to practice conduct that is conducive to satisfactory group living. Through the development of good work habits and favorable attitudes toward their associates and their work, they recognize and appreciate the interdependence of individuals. Through activities which improve learning and living not only in school but also in the community, they observe the relationship between school and home, between school and community.

MEETING THE NEEDS OF THE PUPILS

Teachers in the classrooms described here do not concern themselves solely with the problem of progressive procedures versus conventional or traditional procedures but, rather, with problems which involve the total growth and development of children. Each teacher considers a child's needs in relation to his individual ability and personality. The focusing point of both teachers is identical: the *child* and *how* he learns. This *how* directs the *what* of teaching. Although the procedures may differ, the same objectives are in the minds of both teachers; the same outcomes are sought.

Teacher Planning. The basic difference between the procedures set up by Miss Brown and Mrs. White stems from the basic differences in teacher planning. Miss Brown, who utilizes controlled informality as the keynote of her teaching, directs her planning skillfully to provide constant guidance for children toward self-direction. She weighs the effort to be expended against results to be gained. She finds that efficiency and effectiveness are most successfully attained by planning in units. The children share in the planning and gain skill in self-direction and self-evaluation as they carry out their plans.

Mrs. White, a teacher who uses formal organization as the keynote of her teaching, directs her planning skillfully to stimulate and maintain the children's interest in work planned and suggested by *her*. This teacher finds that efficiency and effectiveness are most successfully attained through the planning of a systematic sequence of lesson-by-lesson learnings in the various subject-matter areas. But she misses no opportunity that may arise during these lessons to develop good character and good work habits in her pupils.

Both types of teachers meet the immediate needs of their pupils. One extends the horizons of children by providing experiences that develop self-direction and encourage the assuming of responsibility. The other recognizes and takes advantage of opportunities as they present themselves.

The teacher who utilizes the technique of unit planning does not neglect the tool subjects. She guides the children to a realization of the importance of these subjects. She directs the pupils toward continual self-evaluation that serves as a guide for practice in needed areas. And the teacher who plans lesson-by-lesson programs directs the practice in tool subjects as she evaluates each individual's need for such practice. Both types of teachers can be equally effective and successful in accomplishing the aims and objectives of sound education.

Learning by Doing. Elementary-school classrooms, such as those described above, form natural settings for the inculcation of fundamental principles of democratic living and learning. Children must learn to feel the power and glory of such principles. They must have faith in them. Children living and working in classrooms such as these *do* have faith in democracy. By living and working together harmoniously, by sharing experiences and responsibilities, they are constantly putting these great principles into practice. They realize that the democratic society about which they study is really their own way of life, an actuality with which they are familiar. They learn to appreciate, respect, and evaluate each individual and his contribution to the society of the classroom. They learn to take their places in various situations, leading in some activities and following in others, but always contributing their abilities and best efforts to the group. They respect authority because they respect individuals. They understand the need for sound and firm leadership, for regulations and learnings which are essential to wholesome group living. Most important of all, these children learn to assume responsibility for their decisions, whether they make the decisions as individuals or as members of the group.

AN EXPANDING CURRICULUM

These classrooms provide rich and varied opportunities for group living through the type of curriculum they develop. A curriculum which is broad and inclusive embraces in its scope the children, the teacher, the school facilities, the instructional materials, and the community resources. A study of the development of education in this country reveals the amazing expansion of the school curriculum.

Major Objectives of Education. The major objectives of American schools have remained almost constant: to help pupils to become literate and to provide them with opportunities to acquire in school those desirable learnings they are unable to acquire as well in any other place.

School Environment. In the earlier schools of America, education was acquired through arduous drill and memorization of facts. These early schools were almost devoid of instructional materials and interests associated with the daily lives of children.

The teacher was there to teach pupils a specific kind and amount of subject matter. A few textbooks were her only tools. The classroom was bleak; discipline was rigid; the curriculum was narrow and limited.

In the schools of today, instructional materials and interests relate to many aspects of the daily lives of children. The teacher's role is to teach *children*. Critical thinking, self-discipline, and self-direction are considered more important than the memorization of facts alone. A specially designed school environment utilizes the resources of the community. The curriculum is broad.

Life Situations. Years ago, when society and life were more simple, children did not need a specially designed school environment, for much was learned from the world itself. Many of the children attending school participated actively in providing for the general welfare of the family. These young folk helped to provide food, shelter, and clothing. They often assumed important roles in family planning and in carrying out these plans. They learned through practical experience. They were surrounded by experiences tangible and important to them. These children gained much of their learning through direct observation and active participation.

Longfellow's *The Village Blacksmith* illustrates the type of learning situation which was available to children of a century ago:

> And children coming home from school
> Look in at the open door;
> They love to see the flaming forge,
> And hear the bellows roar,
>
> . . . .

The blacksmith then welcomed his young visitors. He had time to answer their questions and to give them the experience of handling tools. The baker, the shoemaker, and other neighborhood workers were also sources of firsthand information for the children of yesteryear. The doors of the shops of these workers always remained open.

Most children of today do not have opportunities to share actively in providing for their own daily needs. Too seldom do they enjoy the privilege of observing the relationship between individual effort and their own general welfare. As they come "home from school" they may pass a city dairy, a barbershop, a busy garage, a dry-cleaning establishment, or a match factory. Do they stop and "look in at the open door?" They do not. Why? Do today's adults express less interest in children? What forces have closed these doors?

Because of technological advances, children of today have become consumers. They depend upon the efforts of others for their food, clothing, and shelter and for their transporation, communication, and recreation. They accept the results of the efforts of others, for the most part, without question. The association between their needs and the sources of supply for meeting these needs does not arouse any appreciable amount of curiosity in today's children. As a matter of fact, many of today's adults possess little understanding of the close association that exists between their needs and the ways in which these needs are met. Much of this is taken for granted today.

Motivating Forces. The parents of many children of early America were self-employed. They could observe firsthand the direct relationship between the amount and quality of their work and the welfare of their families. If they worked efficiently and conscientiously they could provide their families not only with daily necessities but also with assurance of future security. This relationship between effort expended and family welfare was recognized by the children as well as the adults of the family. The appreciation of this relationship was a strong motivating force for the development of habits of industry and conscientious work.

Today mass production and the assembly line have made a wide variety of material things available to people at home and abroad. But the very nature of industry demands many individualized and specialized forms of labor. Industry requires special skills which the workers practice over and over again. Only the unusual worker discovers for himself the relationship between the operation he performs and the finished product to which his efforts contribute. Industry trains the worker of today to be efficient, to be ever-conscious of safety measures, and to produce effectively a part of a whole—a whole which the worker himself may not appreciate until he purchases the commodity in a downtown store. It is, therefore, the responsibility of schools to provide for children experiences through which they may discover and appreciate the interdependence of individuals within a society and the dependence of human beings upon the resources of the community.

Apprenticeship. As the children of earlier days in America grew older, doors were opened for them to learn trades. A boy or girl who wished to learn a trade apprenticed himself or herself to a skilled worker employed in a craft in which he or she was interested. The apprentice served for a long period of time—a period of private, individualized instruction, with the skilled worker serving as the tutor and the apprentice as the pupil. Step by step the trade was learned and practiced. And no apprentice was permitted to take his place as an independent worker until he was considered completely qualified by the master craftsman with whom he worked. Even the professional men of earlier days trained young people in the basic principles of law, medicine, dentistry, and pharmacy.

Today doors are open for boys and girls to learn trades, but they are the doors of trade schools, where vocational skills and techniques are taught in conjunction with academic subjects. In communities without trade schools, boys and girls may find opportunities to learn their trades in shops or factories. But the professions today are taught only in the colleges and universities.

A Slow Process. For a long time, the sole aim of education was to make children literate. The curriculum was narrow and limited. This was due partly to the fact that for generations the home and community provided the opportunities for learning the skills of homemaking, farming, trades, and professions. One reason that home and community sufficed was that technological developments and social change were slow in being achieved. Moreover, the public demands upon education were not great. The mastery of subject matter gained by arduous drill and memorization remained, therefore, the primary objective of the curriculum for generations. Gradually, however, the changing and increasing complexity of patterns of living demanded a shift in emphasis—from subject matter to children. Acceptance of this change provided the impetus for broadening the school curriculum. The actual development of a broader curriculum proved to be a slow process.

Justifiable Change. All school systems, before adopting changes and expanding their curricula, must make certain that changes are needed. Changes should not be made unless the new order gives evidence of proving more effective than the old. Change should produce more good for more people.

Society and education both dictate change. Society establishes the pattern of a culture. An altered cultural pattern may indicate the need for revising the curriculum. When society indicates the need for change, the problem is usually carefully studied before the curriculum is altered or expanded, for changes in attitude toward new skills and new procedures in education evolve slowly. However, a revision eventually comes, because society does not dictate change until technological and scientific progress has so influenced the pattern of living that curriculum changes are essential. Education itself also dictates change. Schools bear serious responsibility for taking the lead in effecting changes in curriculum—changes which may strongly influence cultural patterns. Sometimes the impetus for change comes from the societal cultural pattern, sometimes from education.

Weaving a Pattern. Teachers of elementary schools now realize that the ever-changing social and economic pattern of living provides the warp through which the woof of modern education must be woven. The first and most important task faced by the schools is that of helping children understand that the quantity and quality of *their* work affect their own welfare. Children should have opportunities to help plan their work—what they will learn, how they will participate, and the scale for evaluating their work. This privilege of sharing in planning should prove to children that the advantages an individual receives from life are in proportion to the contribution he makes to it. Children must learn the fallacy of attempting to get something for nothing.

The Dignity of Work. As a part of their program of education, children should participate in activities which help them to understand the relationship between individual effort and general welfare. In one classroom, for example, children listed the occupations of their parents. They studied ways in which each parent contributed to the individual welfare of each child in the class and to the general welfare of the community. They went so far as to evaluate each parent's contribution to the national welfare. (These occupations were listed and studied with no parent's name attached.) This study helped the children to realize the dignity and importance of all kinds of work and services. Another class studied about the many different kinds of workers who help to supply each of their primary needs—food, shelter, and clothing— and their secondary needs—transportation, communication, and recreation.

Understanding Relationships. A study of the results of curtailment of imported goods helped a group of elementary-school children to realize the importance of satisfactory international relations, as well as good domestic relationships. A discussion of the effects of a strike among the workers in a major industry proved to one group of children that unsatisfactory relationships between labor and management have far-reaching effects upon the general welfare and the welfare of individuals.

Group planning, studying in groups, and making group decisions have many advantages, but the "group mentality" presents one grave danger for schools to consider—the danger that individuals may try to evade responsibility for action to which they, as members of a group, are committed by group decision. A group-conscious society must not serve as a force which overlooks moral obligations and commits itself to policies opposed to the general welfare. Because of the danger involved when many individuals make group decisions which would never be made by individuals alone, today's schools must emphasize individual as well as group responsibilities which involve moral values.

Future Patterns. The future patterns which education seems destined to weave will depend upon the number of doors which curricula open to fulfill the needs of the children of today and tomorrow. These patterns must remain steadfast to the primary aims of education—to make children literate, to give children educational experiences not provided elsewhere, and to assume responsibility for strengthening those qualities of good character and good citizenship emphasized by the home, the church, and government institutions.

The school must mold the parts of its curriculum to ensure daily results that not only fulfill the immediate needs of children but also prepare them to meet their future needs. This substance consists of those basic skills in the tool subjects which make human beings literate and those social skills which direct them toward harmonious group living.

Illiterate people may function well in a totalitarian regime because their minds are permitted little opportunity to work intelligently. Coercion alone does not force them to follow, but rather, the illiteracy of the masses allows one mind to lead or mislead the many. The social skills involved in understanding one another, respecting human rights, appreciating the contributions made by individuals and by groups, and respecting law and order remain secure in a democracy only when literacy flourishes among the masses. Literacy of the masses remains secure in America only as long as teachers in schools keep foremost in mind the relative importance of the substance necessary for the nation's children.

Building an Effective Citizenry. Teaching children the fundamental principles of democracy proves futile in a school environment devoid of democratic practice. Respect for and understanding of authority, law and order, and a knowledge of the individual's responsibility toward himself, his community, and his country become the dominant factors in building an effective citizenry. Providing an environment that lays the foundation for this effective citizenry is the task of the elementary school.

SUMMARY

This chapter explains the many experiences that influence the nature of elementary education. It emphasizes the fact that in an atmosphere of wholesome democratic living, children prepare themselves for group living in a complex society. They gain skill in the tool subjects and learn to evaluate personal skill and progress in the mastery of these subjects. They develop special abilities and interests. They learn to work and play together. Through a careful blending of these learnings, children develop those qualities essential to the opening wide of the doors which lead to abundant opportunities for fruitful living.

Physical education provides many opportunities for the enrichment of living that improves personal and general welfare. The following chapter presents these opportunities.

QUESTIONS AND TOPICS FOR DISCUSSION

1. How does the development of good work habits and favorable attitudes toward one's associates affect group living?

2. What things does the successful teacher emphasize?

3. What is the basic difference between traditional education and progressive education?

4. Describe the methods of program planning which are suitable for use in elementary schools.

5. What is meant by extending the elementary-school curriculum?

6. What are the major objectives of education today?

7. How has the child's environment influenced educational practices?

8. What justifies curriculum change?

9. Of what does the *substance* referred to in this chapter consist?

10. What dominant factors in the building of an effective citizenry are considered in the elementary school today?

SUGGESTED ACTIVITY UNIT

Plan a unit of work through which a group of children will realize the number of people involved in one simple event: for example, receiving a valentine via postal service. This unit will vary in its scope according to the age and previous experiences of the children in the group. It will include not only an appreciation of the work of postal employees but also a realization of the workers necessary for obtaining and manufacturing the materials used in the valentine itself and in the writing utensils.

A birthday, Christmas, New Year, St. Patrick's Day, or any other holiday may be substituted for Valentine's Day.

Before planning a unit, the teacher should make a thorough study of the techniques of unit teaching. Suggested references may be found at the end of Part One.

2. Enter Physical Education

Every subject in the curriculum should make a genuine contribution to the total school program. Conversely, every subject should possess a uniqueness that sets it apart from all others in such a way that the effect would be deleterious if the subject were not included. This chapter demonstrates the ways in which physical education, when wisely planned and carried on, fulfills both these requirements. Physical education interests for boys and girls of all age levels provide motivation for many worthwhile units of work in the classroom. The far-reaching effects of this important school subject are illustrated in the sections that follow.

THE CORE OF A UNIT

A reading group in Room 19 in Madison School had just completed a discussion of the story "Josie's Home Run." The enthusiasm of the members of this group had been so contagious that the other children in the classroom had listened and even contributed to the discussion. Moreover, the class had important plans for this particular morning—plans related to the activities described in the story of Josie's triumph. These children hoped that they would soon have experiences similar to those of the girl who became a member of a baseball team.

It was indeed a great day for the children in Room 19—a climax to two weeks of work and play. It was the day when two softball teams were to be selected. These two teams would play a series of games on the same days that the World Series baseball games were being played.

Preparation and Practice. The children had prepared carefully for this day. They had learned the rules of the game and had

18

practiced the skills of pitching, catching, batting, and fielding until they knew their individual strengths and weaknesses. Many children had confidence in their own abilities and skills, but each child wondered whether the other children in the class realized these skills. Each one was thinking, "Shall I be chosen to play on one of the teams?"

Dick, unable to control his eagerness another minute after the reading group had ended its discussion of the story, asked Miss Gray if they might please get down to business and choose the baseball teams.

Beverly asked, "How shall we choose the teams? Shall we vote? How many girls shall we choose? Who . . . ?"

Jim interrupted, "You can't just vote for a baseball team, Beverly. We want best players, not most popular people. It doesn't matter how many girls there are on the team if they can play ball like Josie."

"We can think of best players when we vote, can't we?" asked Jack.

Setting Standards. "Wouldn't it be helpful to list on the board some qualifications for good ball players?" suggested Miss Gray.

An emphatic "yes" resulted in Mary Ann's acting as secretary and listing the criteria which the group considered essential to good ball playing. These criteria included good sportsmanship, clear thinking, and a sense of team play, as well as quick acting, alertness, resourcefulness, skill in pitching, batting, catching, and fielding. Knowledge of the rules of the game, good judgment, and fairness were listed as criteria for the selection of umpires.

Application of Standards. Criteria dictated by the children and written by Mary Ann were considered carefully as the class voted for members of the two teams and for the umpires. Some children were named to warm up the relief pitchers. Others were chosen to sit on the bench ready to serve as possible pinch hitters. There were scorekeepers and recorders whose responsibility was to keep a play-by-play record of each game. Every child enjoyed the series, especially if his team of Yankees or Dodgers won a game on the same day that the baseball champions of the same name won a victory.

Motivation through Current Interest. This informal, enthusiastic approach to a timely interest manifests itself time and time again in elementary classrooms throughout the year. Such interest and enthusiasm often stem from physical education. Appropriate activity often contains sufficient stimulus to satisfy the objectives of skill development; in addition, it provides a depth and scope of related activities that encourage the use of academic skills. Teachers channel the interests of children in these activities to serve as motivation for broader learnings and deeper appreciations.

Related Activities. In the foregoing activity the teacher directed the interests of the children to stimulate their desire to learn how to figure batting averages and percentages of games won, how to describe the game play by play, either orally or in written form, and how to correlate the skills, special abilities, and batting averages of favorite players. Many children did research on the records of players of other years. They read biographical stories about Babe Ruth, Lou Gehrig, Ty Cobb, Rabbit Maranville, Jackie Robinson, Joe DiMaggio, Ted Williams, Roy Campanella, and others. They presented oral reports to other classes. Some children made baseball booklets and sent them to children who were ill at home or in hospitals.

Vital Learnings. What better way can be found to learn to express oneself than to speak or write about something of universal interest? Would it be possible to find a more exciting way to obtain practice in figuring percentages than to compute batting averages? How could the habit of reading for recreation be more easily developed than by reading stories like "Josie's Home Run" or newspaper articles that describe ball games or present information about ball players? These experiences provide vital learnings. And through the development and use of skills in physical education activities, children realize that satisfactory performance in any endeavor requires a careful training period, whether it be in throwing a ball or in learning how to add.

CONTRIBUTING TO THE TOTAL PROGRAM

If carefully planned and taught, physical education, probably more than any other school subject, can serve as an important part of the total school program without becoming so integrated that it loses its identity. In the foregoing activity the subject of physical education provided the motivation for learning new academic and physical skills and for improving skills already acquired in physical education, arithmetic, reading, spelling, and language. The skills in each area were acquired and practiced separately, but they were related in interest and substance. Each subject contributed its "kit" of tools to the successful completion of a unit of instruction, the core of which was physical education.

Modern educators look for deeper and broader outcomes than the mere acquisition of skills. The classroom teacher must understand that there is something more important than a game to be played, new steps of a dance to be learned, or an exercise to be performed. She must know how and why this subject is related to others in the curriculum and what possibilities and opportunities exist for the subject to contribute to the total growth and development of the child. Then, and only then, should she plan the teaching unit around that subject, using it as a core.

Physical Education as an Indicator. It is an established fact that children must be physically ready for work. If teachers would use as indicators the physical reactions of their pupils rather than the hands of the clock, fewer unsuccessful learning situations would result. There must be physical readiness for concentration and physical endurance for sustained attention. Restlessness and/ or inattentiveness usually indicate that a child has reached the peak of his attention endurance or that he is not ready to concentrate. Often a release of only a few minutes from a tedious task relaxes a child and makes him ready to resume work. Pupils may obtain this release by leaving their places and moving freely around the room for a short period of time. Such relaxation does not require the direction or the permission of the teacher. Children should be free to satisfy their personal needs independently. They should, however, be taught to use good judgment in such practice so that other pupils are not disturbed or distracted.

Whenever a teacher senses class tension or restlessness, she should recognize the need for a brief period of group activity or rest. Relaxation periods should not be regulated by bells which announce that all children from one section of the building shall visit the toilets and drinking fountains and then proceed to the playground until another bell calls them back to their classrooms. In many elementary schools, recess, so called, is a forgotten practice. Periods of relaxation and recreational activity are provided whenever the need for them is indicated. Children's behavior is the best indicator of the need for a change of pace in the school program. Caring for personal needs such as making use of sanitary facilities is an individual matter and should be attended to as such. Physical education periods and play periods should be planned in connection with units of work or to fit the general needs of each teacher's group of pupils.

Mind, Body, Spirit. The classroom teacher recognizes the developmental relationship of mind, body, and spirit. She sees, as well, the contributions that physical education makes to the achievement of total fitness. Children who demonstrate vigor, enthusiasm, and good character traits in their practice of physical education activities usually participate in other learning situations with greater success than do those who do not seem to possess these qualities. Physical education, for this reason, is not limited to "periods of activity." It is, rather, a way or means of education which utilizes the medium of physical activity and which is a part of the total program of child growth and development. Its aim is to contribute to the all-round development of the child. Its objectives point toward that goal.

OBJECTIVES OF PHYSICAL EDUCATION

The objectives of physical education, stated generally, include (1) the development and use of organic power, (2) the development of neuromuscular skills, (3) the establishment of attitudes favorable to physical activity, especially play, and (4) the establishment of desirable standards of conduct. Specifically, the program of physical education in elementary schools attempts to develop in children such qualities as strength, endurance, agility, and good posture; to contribute to efficient body mechanics; and to maintain a balance of activity and rest, work and recreation. Specific purposes of physical education activities are to help children (1) become proficient in the skills of running, walking, dodging, jumping, and gauging moving objects and (2) become acquainted with and efficient in a variety of activities, especially team games, individual sports, stunts, and rhythmic activities.

Physical Fitness. The term *physical fitness* is quite generally applied to the effective functioning of the total organism—physical, mental, social, and emotional. One essential factor pertaining to this total-fitness interpretation is developing a strong and well-coordinated body. Physical education is signally important because optimum child growth and development naturally induce an appreciable amount of physical activity. However, strong muscles, good posture, and endurance develop only as the result of well-planned physical activity—activity adapted to the needs and capacities of those participating in the program of physical education.

Social Skills. The objectives just discussed point toward the goal for which all education strives—an enlightened, responsible citizenry, whose members conduct themselves in socially acceptable ways and enjoy wholesome recreation. Children learn to conduct themselves in socially acceptable ways if they have opportunities to learn, through games and other group activities, to act in sportsmanlike ways, to work and play for the common good, and to respect the personalities of their classmates. This process requires opportunities to exercise self-control in emotionally tense activities, as well as practice in games in which players must react quickly and under pressure. Children need to learn, through participation in dancing, swimming, and other sports, how to enjoy themselves and to be at ease in a variety of social situations.

Wholesome Recreation. Today's children enjoy wholesome recreation only if they have learned to include in their daily lives activities that are creative, relaxing, or stimulating, and thus can draw upon a fund of recreational interests, knowledges, appreciations, and skills. Thus it is evident that a broad program of physical education does not limit its purpose to the development of only one factor in physical fitness, important as that one factor may be. Rather, it provides for youth a widely varied program of activities which helps them (1) to establish wholesome associations, (2) to assume responsibility for individual and group decisions, and (3) to develop efficiency in recreational and social skills.

A Road to Understanding. Physical education, in harmony with other areas of education, helps children to understand their own life situations and to develop skills and techniques to meet these situations. They learn to face reality, to make decisions after carefully weighing all the factors pertinent to the situation, and, finally, to accept responsibility for their decisions and their subsequent actions. Opportunities to develop these skills and techniques are abundant in physical education. It is the responsibility of teachers to provide these opportunities. Under the careful guidance of intelligent and understanding teachers, opportunities are provided for many experiences that broaden and enrich the children's mode of living, creating in them the fabric out of which patterns of self-direction are formed and thus helping them adjust their lives to their environment. Within these experiences the teacher must help children to develop definite skills, to form desirable attitudes, and to appreciate broad concepts.

It is not enough to present a game situation. Natural capacities for throwing, catching, fielding, running, or other neuromuscular skills can be developed only through *learning* these skills and having practice in improving them. Proper attitudes toward play and toward participants in play can only be developed by engaging often in activities which offer opportunities to express these attitudes and by learning correct responses to these same attitudes in others. Concepts of game strategy can be gained only through careful teaching. Success in any endeavor results from carefully building up and developing potentialities.

Self-discipline. Physical education helps to develop self-discipline in children and conditions them to accept discipline imposed by others. In physical education the advantages of good discipline are obvious. Good discipline requires that each person know just what is expected of him, that each person know exactly what he can do and what he cannot do. In a good discipline situation, children know the limits of their freedom and can depend upon these limits being present at all times. Trouble arises when children are given more freedom than they can handle.

In physical education, more than in any other area of education, natural situations for good discipline are plentiful, and in a well-planned physical education lesson freedom seldom exceeds the child's capacity to handle it. This is true mainly because in physical education the results of good discipline (or bad discipline) are immediately evident and are usually recognized by the children themselves. Good discipline in physical education contributes valuably toward building a balance between competition and cooperation.

Satisfying a Need. It is a recognized fact that children's personalities are affected by their success or failure in satisfying their emotional needs—their needs to achieve, to be wanted, to gain status, to be approved by others, and to be included in the group. In what subject area can teachers help children to satisfy these needs better than in physical education? Most children can achieve success to a greater or lesser degree in some type of physical education activity. Children are quick to show their approval and appreciation of another's success in a game, sport, rhythm, or dance. It is fun to receive commendation from one's classmates for a good catch, a home run, a basket scored, or a dance step skillfully executed.

In instances where success in physical education is not achieved, the causes for failure come to light—causes which may affect every area of education. During recreation or game periods, a teacher may detect results of structural inheritance that decrease a child's aptitude for physical education activity; or a teacher may notice changing bodily functions or signs of temporary illness. The alert teacher realizes that an alteration in a child's fundamental mood may reflect a change in his vital functions. Thus, detection of even slight trouble often results in immediate care of a minor ailment or careful attention to more serious defects which might pass unnoticed during the academic educative process. Many defects can be corrected, and in the case of incorrectible defects, the school should help children become adjusted to their handicaps and learn to compensate for them. Thus physical education is instrumental in helping all children develop to their optimum.

UNIQUENESS OF PHYSICAL EDUCATION

In a time of great social change and cultural confusion, physical education can do much to salvage a principle of unity which brings order out of chaos. Physical education provides many opportunities for children to do things together, to learn skills, to think, to plan, to execute, and to evaluate definite results which are of significant benefit to society. Abilities such as these are the essence of the good life, which is the goal of true education.

Doubtless, the fun and enjoyment inherently associated with physical education enable this program to surpass all other subjects in providing wholesome opportunity for sound education. Why is it that children, when properly guided, always anticipate the physical education period with such pleasure and feel cheated when it is omitted? Is it because they do just as they please during these lessons? No. It is because one of physical education's greatest contributions is to provide experiences in which children have fun. Moreover, these experiences can be transferred to the daily lives of children outside of school. Physical skills are learned, attitudes are established, social graces are developed; but first and foremost, a good time is enjoyed by all. Herein lies the uniqueness of physical education.

SUMMARY

It is evident that physical education makes a worthwhile contribution to the total school program. As a core of a unit, physical education can provide the motivation for learning new physical and academic skills and for improving skills already learned in other subject-matter areas. Observation during physical education lessons proves that physical education serves as an indicator of physical readiness for concentration and sustained attention. It serves as an indicator of the welfare of children.

It is also evident that physical education makes a worthwhile contribution to the total fitness of the individual. It helps children to develop physically, socially, emotionally, and mentally. A well-planned program of physical education satisfies many of the needs of the participants.

It is vitally important that teachers be cognizant of the changing physical, social, emotional, and mental characteristics of children of different age groups. It is also important that teachers realize that some principles of planning and procedure are adaptable to all age groups. Chapter 3 explains these principles and procedures.

QUESTIONS AND TOPICS FOR DISCUSSION

1. How does physical education contribute to the total school program?

2. Plan a unit of instruction, the core of which is a physical education activity.

3. How does observation gained in a physical education period influence teaching and learning?

4. What are the aims and purposes of physical education in the elementary school?

5. What does the term *physical fitness* mean?

6. What objectives does a teacher consider when planning a program of physical education?

7. How do these objectives contribute to the goals of total education?

8. What does a broad and comprehensive program of physical education include?

9. Wherein does the uniqueness of physical education lie?

SUGGESTED ACTIVITY UNIT

Plan a unit to culminate in a program for United Nations Day. Preparation for such a program should include a study of interesting historical facts, customs, games, sports, and dances of different member countries of the United Nations. The material to be used must be carefully evaluated and selected.

This unit may be planned as a class project or school project, the basis upon which it is planned determining the depth and scope of the project.

Pan-American Day or some national holiday may be substituted for United Nations Day.

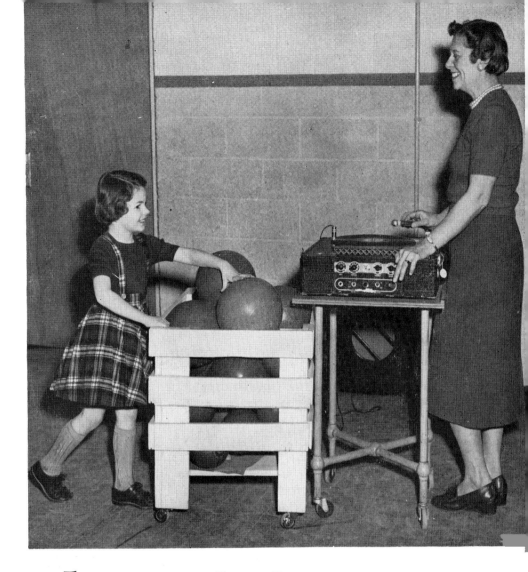

3. Setting the Stage:
Planning and Procedures
Adaptable to All
Age Groups

Although educators acknowledge the fact that individuals within a group differ, they also agree that children of a specific age group demonstrate *like* as well as *unlike* characteristics. Educators therefore find it possible to develop programs for groups of children rather than for individuals. However, individuals who deviate from the average must be considered when any such program is being planned.

PLANNING THE PROGRAM

The competent teacher of any age group directs the interests and enthusiasms of children into channels that satisfy their physical needs, challenge their mental capabilities, and increase their emotional stability. When a teacher organizes a physical education program, he considers not only the characteristics common to most children of a particular age group but also the variations within the group. He may organize a program in which he uses physical education as a core or a supplement to a unit of work; or he may organize a program of carefully planned daily activity.

Using physical education as a core or a supplement to a unit of work requires skillful planning. The needs, capabilities, and interests of the children concerned must receive careful consideration before an attempt is made to correlate or integrate physical education with a unit of work in any other subject-matter area.

Long-range Planning. A wise teacher makes no attempt to introduce physical education activities into a unit which does not by nature lend itself to correlation or integration with these activities. Unit planning alone sometimes fails to provide the opportunity to organize a balanced program of activities which provides for a systematic development of new skills and a satisfactory retention of skills already learned. Therefore, the teacher should realize the essential value of careful, long-range planning for the program of physical education.

30

Necessity for Balance. A teacher should be cognizant and ever-conscious of the value of balance among the types of physical education activity taught to the children in elementary school. An equitable distribution of time should be made in order to ensure this balance in the program. This distribution varies according to the needs and interests of the specific group for whom the program is planned or of the individuals within the group. However, many teachers best achieve their objectives by weekly planning, which often results in delegating two physical education periods each week to play activities or games, two periods to rhythms and dance, and one to conditioning or self-testing activities. Tables 1 and 2 on the following page illustrate the plan just described and are suggested as a guide in program planning. It in no way contradicts the advocacy of an integrated program that is planned by a skilled teacher. It is merely a guide for the inexperienced or unskilled teacher.

There may be weeks when it seems advisable to use all five daily physical education periods for teaching one type of activity; or certain factors may render it desirable to change an activity planned for a particular day. The weather is a factor to consider. When conditions justify outdoor play, the emphasis at any season will be placed upon outdoor games. Likewise, during the winter season, when in some sections of the country the weather is cold and stormy, rhythms and other suitable indoor activities should receive the emphasis. This apparent overemphasis on outdoor activities during the warm months and on indoor activities during the colder months provides in itself a program balance in certain geographical areas. In those sections where there is less variation in climate it is possible to balance outdoor and indoor activities throughout the entire school year.

Flexibility is desirable and essential in order that the program meet the changing needs of children. Only by being ever-conscious of this may teachers effectively cope with behavior problems which sometimes are the result of weather conditions, current interests, or changing classroom situations. The absence of several children in the group is a factor that may prevent the successful teaching or optimum enjoyment of some activities.

For the success of the physical education program, then, the teacher must consider a balance among games, rhythms, dances,

Table 1. *Suggested Time Distribution for Physical Education*
(In minutes per week)

Activity	Kindergarten	Lower grades (1–4)	Upper grades (5–8)
Instruction and practice	150	150	200
Play periods	150	75	100
Relaxation periods	150	75	—
Total program	450	300	300

Table 2. *Suggested Weekly Schedule of Physical Education Activities*

Grades	Monday	Tuesday	Wednesday	Thursday	Friday
	Outdoor activities program				
Lower	Large-group games	Small-group games	Large-group games	Small-group games	Singing games
Upper	Team games .... Fall season				
	Team games and track and field........... Spring season				
	Indoor activities program				
Lower	Games	Rhythms	Games	Rhythms	Stunts
Upper	Gymnastics and games Skills	Rhythms Dance	Gymnastics and games Skills	Rhythms Dance	Small-group games

and conditioning and self-testing activities; he must also bear in mind the essential values of indoor and outdoor activities, and the relative importance of activities for large groups, small groups, and individuals. Suggested seasonal guides are included in Table 3. These guides ensure a balanced program of physical activity.

Table 3. Seasonal Guides for the Physical Education Program

Age level	Play unit	Conditioning	Rhythmical activities	Self-testing
		Fall		
5–8 *	Small-group games Self-directed play Simple ball skills Catching, Throwing, Ball bouncing Tag games Relays (8-year-olds)	Skills of locomotion Walking, running Hopping, jumping Galloping, leaping Jumping, sliding Bending, stretching Twisting, whirling	Characterizations Singing games Fundamental rhythms Creative response	Outdoor play on apparatus Simple tumbling Individual stunts (little or no apparatus)
9–12 †	Small-group games Circle games with balls Soccer, baseball, basketball, volleyball skills Skill drills Team games Related activities	Review of skills learned in lower elementary school Exercises for development of correct body mechanics Posture exercises	Creative rhythms Folk and traditional dance steps Waltz Schottische Polka Dance formations Square dance Quadrilles Reels	Individual and couple stunts Tumbling (moderately difficult)
		Winter		
5–8 *	Snow games (if climate permits) Large-group games Small-group games Tag games Relays (8-year-olds)	Combined axial and locomotor movements Posture exercises Walking Sitting Standing Exercises for development of various muscle groups	Simple folk dancing Singing games Creative response Dramatic rhythms	Tumbling and couple stunts Activity on apparatus Bowling marbles

* Refer to Chapters 5 and 6.
† Refer to Chapters 7 and 8.

Table 3. Seasonal Guides for the Physical Education Program (continued)

9–12 †	Team games Large-group games Small-group games	Posture exercises Standing Walking Sitting Posture relays Foot exercises	Folk dances Square dances Country dances Social dances Quadrilles Reels	Combatives Stunt-and- partner relays Sidewalk games Shuffleboard

Spring

5–8 °	Sidewalk games Small-group games Large-group games	Exercises for development of correct posture in lifting Simple calisthenics Posture exercises Standing Sitting Walking	Dramatic rhythms Singing games Folk dances Creative response	Simple pyramids Stunts Outdoor play on appara- tus Rope skipping Simple games of skill
9–12 †	Tag and relay variations Team games and related activities Track and field events	Marching forma- tions Simple calis- thenics Posture exercises Standing Sitting Walking	Folk dances Reels Quadrilles Square dances Social dances	Rope-skipping variations Track and field events Outdoor activity on apparatus Stunt relays

° Refer to Chapters 5 and 6.
† Refer to Chapters 7 and 8.

The following are among the requisites of good program planning:

1. Know your children.

2. Be familiar with the characteristics of the age group with which you are associated.

3. Plan a balanced program which will suit these characteristics.

4. Allow for program flexibility.

5. Provide for expansion and retention in the skills area.

6. Provide an atmosphere conducive to good learning.

7. Foster a spirit of happiness and security that will lead to good mental hygiene.

Lesson Planning. After long-range planning, a teacher must make specific lesson plans. The teacher who conducts a program of physical education made up of units of instruction needs an over-all list of objectives. These objectives may be compiled from the requirements given in Chapters 5 to 8 for the development of skills in each age group.

Plausible correlation of these skills within the complete unit must be carefully planned. As the teacher plans the unit, he should make provision for the instruction and practice which are essential to the development of skills. Tables 4 and 5 on the following pages suggest weekly plans for the physical education program. These plans are intended merely as guides for the teacher who needs help in determining the types and purposes of activities suitable for the different age levels. The teacher constantly keeps in mind the unit in its entirety and the separate lessons which contribute to the completion of the unit. Examples of unit planning may be found in each of the following four chapters.

A teacher who is not conducting a unit of instruction, but is planning the program of physical education on the basis of a series of separate lessons, should compile a list of weekly objectives for his pupils to achieve. He should plan a series of lessons that provides for a sequential progression of skills through widely varied activities. He should always be prepared to change the type of activity when weather conditions or the needs or interests of children make such a change desirable.

The outlines below contain lesson plans and suggestions for teaching specific physical education activities. The following outline presents a suggested lesson plan for seven- and eight-year-olds in apparatus activity:

A. Objectives
    1. To help children develop balance and increase agility.
    2. To provide vigorous activity which will result in strengthening of muscles.
    3. To help children develop self-confidence.
    4. To provide fun and exercise.
    5. To teach children to take turns.
    6. To satisfy children's desire to climb.
B. Teaching Suggestions
    1. Swinging forward and backward on swings.

    a. Have children grasp ropes firmly.

    b. Keep children who are waiting for turns away from swings.

    c. Do not permit standing or climbing on swings.

    d. Permit only one child at a time on swings.

Table 4. Weekly Plan for the Five- to Eight-year-olds *

Monday	Tuesday	Wednesday	Thursday	Friday
		Five-year-olds		
Large-block play Self-directed play	Skills of locomotion Walking Running Hopping Jumping	Small-group games Rope jumping Bounce ball Find Me	Characterizations Animals Toys Singing games Muffin Man Looby Loo	Outdoor play on apparatus Slide Jungle-gym Swings
		Six-year-olds		
Simple ball skills Throwing, catching Dodging Dodge ball	Skills of locomotion Variations in tempo and directions	Small-group games Toss and Bounce Beanbag in the Triangle	Characterizations Giants Fairies Witches Singing games A-hunting We Will Go Punchinello	Outdoor play on apparatus Low bar Horizontal ladder
		Seven-year-olds		
Small-group games I Say Stoop	Skills of locomotion Patterns of rhythmic movement	Simple ball skills Skills of serving and batting Bat ball	Characterizations Machines and forces of nature Singing games The Thread Follows the Needle Rig-a-Jig-Jig	Outdoor play on apparatus Variations (emphasis on form and skill)

* Refer to Chapters 5 and 6.

Table 5. Weekly Plan for the Nine- to Twelve-year-olds *

Monday	Tuesday	Wednesday	Thursday	Friday
		Eight-year-olds		
Large-group games (mass)	Apparatus activity and calisthenics	Folk dances	Stunt relays	Large-group games
		Nine- and Ten-year-olds		
Large-group games (line)	Calisthenics and apparatus activity	Folk dances	Partner relay	Large-group games
		Eleven- and Twelve-year-olds		
Large-group games (mass)	Apparatus activity Posture relays Relays	Folk dances Square dances	Stunt relays and partner relays	Large-group games (mass and line)

* Refer to Chapters 7 and 8.

2. Sliding down slides.
   a. Have children hold handrails firmly and extend legs forward.
   b. See that each child waits for his turn and does not start until the preceding child has completed his slide.
3. Climbing up and down and in and out of squares in a Jungle-gym.
   a. See that children hang on firmly.
   b. Closely supervise children when inverted positions are allowed.
4. Hanging and traveling on a horizontal ladder.
   a. Allow only one child at a time on the ladder.
   b. Teach children to take care in dismounting—to drop easily and to land with bent knees.

The following outline presents a suggested lesson plan in American folk dancing for nine- and ten-year-olds.

A. Objectives
1. To give children an appreciation of American culture.
2. To help children develop a sense of rhythm and an enjoyment of music.
3. To help children develop poise, coordination, and agility.
4. To provide for the social values derived from dancing.
5. To offer an opportunity for development of aesthetic values.
B. Teaching Suggestions
1. Review a familiar dance and the basic steps which appear in this dance ("O Susannah" suggested).
2. Discuss the period in history from which this dance comes.
3. Have children listen to the music.
4. Teach the dance by phrases, and as each part is learned, combine it with the previous part.
5. Do not stay too long on one dance.
6. To stimulate interests, use audio-visual aids, such as dolls, costumes, pictures, and/or diagrams of formations.

THE TEACHING OF SKILLS

Although planning is essential to successful teaching, it represents only one step of the teaching method. There are other equally important steps, one of which, of course, is the actual instruction. The teaching itself and the children's subsequent enjoyment of an activity are a true test of good planning. The following suggestions are intended to serve as a guide to help teachers successfully carry out planned lessons in the teaching of beanbag and ball skills.

Throwing. In one-handed throwing or rolling, the foot opposite the throwing arm is placed forward and more or less pointing toward the target. In all throwing, the eyes are on the target.

A. Two-handed Rolling Between Legs
1. *Equipment*
6-inch rubber ball, volleyball, 8-inch rubber ball
2. *Points of Emphasis*
a. Stand with feet astride, knees bent, back bent, fingers spread.
b. Place hands on either side and slightly behind the ball.

B. One-handed Rolling
1. *Equipment*
   Tennis ball, softball, beanbags, 6-inch rubber ball, 8-inch rubber ball, volleyball
2. *Points of Emphasis*
   a. Place rolling hand under the ball, fingers spread and pointing forward.
   b. Place thumb on top or side of the ball.
   c. Place opposite foot forward (no step).
   d. Keep eyes on the target.
   e. Swing arm back, keeping elbow straight (pendulum).
   f. Release the ball low, bending trunk forward.

C. Two-hand Bounce and Catch
1. *Equipment*
   6-inch rubber ball, 8-inch rubber ball, volleyball
2. *Points of Emphasis*
   a. Place hands on side of the ball at eye level.
   b. In catching, place hands on side of the ball and "give" with the ball.

D. Two-hand Continuous Bounce
1. *Equipment*
   6-inch rubber ball, 8-inch rubber ball, volleyball
2. *Points of Emphasis*
   a. For beginning position, place hands on side of the ball.
   b. Push the ball down.
   c. "Give" with hands as the ball contacts hands, and push down on the ball (no slapping).
   d. The harder the push, the higher the bounce.

E. One-hand Continuous Bounce
Same equipment and points of emphasis as in D above.

F. Two-hand Underhand Toss
1. *Equipment*
   Tennis ball, softball, beanbag, volleyball, soccer ball, 6-inch rubber ball, 8-inch rubber ball
2. *Points of Emphasis*
   a. Stand with feet astride, hands grasping the ball, fingers spread.
   b. Keep eyes on the target.

      c. Bend knees, swing arms back, letting the ball go between knees.

      d. Release the ball on forward swing of arms.

G. One-hand Underhand Toss

  1. *Equipment*

    Tennis ball, softball, beanbag, volleyball, soccer ball, 6-inch rubber ball, 8-inch rubber ball

  2. *Points of Emphasis*

    a. Place foot opposite throwing hand toward the target.

    b. Hold the ball with fingers spread.

    c. Keep eyes on the target.

    d. Bring throwing hand back and up.

    e. Move hand toward the target and follow through to knee level.

    f. Move other foot to position opposite first foot.

    g. Release the ball (high for a high throw, low for a low throw).

H. Overhand Toss from Chest

  1. *Equipment*

    Volleyball, softball, 6-inch rubber ball, 8-inch rubber ball

  2. *Points of Emphasis*

    a. Stand with feet astride, hands grasping the ball, fingers spread and pointing upward, elbows bent.

    b. Keep eyes on the target.

    c. Release the ball by snapping the wrist.

I. Overhand toss—overhead

  1. *Equipment*

    Volleyball, softball, 6-inch rubber ball, 8-inch rubber ball

  2. *Points of Emphasis*

    a. Stand with feet astride, hands grasping the ball overhead, fingers spread and pointing upward.

    b. Keep eyes on the target.

    c. Release the ball by snapping the wrist.

Catching. Eyes are always on the ball. Feet are always apart for balance. Usually fingers are up when balls are caught above the waist and down when balls are caught below the waist. With all balls caught, either on the ground or in the air, the hands must "give" to reduce the shock of impact and thereby reduce fumbles.

A. Catching Rolling Balls

1. *Equipment*

   Softball, 6-inch rubber ball, 8-inch rubber ball, volleyball, soccer ball

2. *Points of Emphasis*

   a. Drop relaxed arms between and slightly in front of legs. Bend elbows slightly for "cushion" effect.

   b. Bend knees and back.

   c. Keep eyes on the ball.

   d. Keeping wrists relaxed, make a large cup for the ball, fingers spread, pointing down and slightly in, palms facing the ball.

B. Catching Rising (Bounding) Balls

1. *Equipment*

   Softball, 6-inch rubber ball, 8-inch rubber ball, volleyball

2. *Points of Emphasis*

   a. Stand with feet about shoulder-width apart. Generally the foot opposite the throwing arm is advanced slightly.

   b. Hold hands out from the body.

   c. Keep eyes on the ball.

   d. Make a large cup for the ball, palms down, fingers spread and pointing forward and slightly up.

   e. "Give" with the ball as it is received.

C. Catching Falling Balls

1. *Equipment*

   Softball, 6-inch rubber ball, 8-inch rubber ball, volleyball, soccer ball

2. *Points of Emphasis*

   a. Extend arms slightly, elbows bent.

   b. Keep eyes on the ball.

   c. Make a large cup to receive the ball, palms up, thumbs out, fingers spread and relaxed.

Observing the following requisites of good teaching will contribute to optimum success in each lesson.

1. Know what you are teaching. If it is a game, know the rules as well as the skills. If it is a dance or stunt, know the steps or the skills involved. If it is a creative rhythm, feel the mood and character of it before presenting it to the children. Whatever the

activity, be ready to demonstrate it or to tell someone else exactly how to do it. Use audio-visual aids as a means of enriching teaching methods. Chapter 4 will amplify these suggestions.

2. Be patient and give suggestions and directions slowly. Be willing to repeat these suggestions and directions until the children understand them. Unless children become thoroughly familiar with an activity they will not enjoy it. Remember the several levels of ability within the group.

3. Arouse in children an enthusiastic attitude toward physical activity.

4. Develop a friendly, cooperative spirit in the group.

5. Let the children know the purpose of the lesson.

6. Allow ample time for practicing skills, so that the children will have confidence when they participate in activities which utilize these skills.

EVALUATION

The third step in teaching is evaluation. This step is as important as planning and teaching, but it should not consume more than its fair share of time. Pupil evaluation of an activity can be accomplished in a brief discussion of the skills learned and the enjoyment experienced. This discussion may take the form of informal conversation among the children themselves, or it may be a teacher-guided discussion. Teacher evaluation is more technical, but need not be too time-consuming. A written knowledge test or a formally organized skill test may serve the purpose; or the teacher may evaluate the lesson by asking himself such questions as (1) What did the children learn? (2) How much fun did they have?

RESPONSIBILITY FOR EQUIPMENT AND PLAY AREA

In addition to planning, teaching, and evaluating lessons or units, a teacher must assume still another responsibility. Unless the necessary equipment and the play area are in suitable condition for use at the time desired, much teaching time is wasted. If the planned program requires the use of balls, the teacher should make certain beforehand that these balls are available and in good condition. Insufficiently inflated balls hinder the learning of skills. If several classes share the equipment all teachers should know the schedule for using it. Arrangements for sharing playrooms, phonographs, phonograph records, balls, beanbags, and all other types of equipment and apparatus should be made prior to the time of the lesson. In the upper grades teachers may delegate this responsibility to reliable pupils; the teacher of young children does best to handle such details personally.

Many elementary schools lack playrooms or gymnasiums. This fact naturally limits the scope of the physical education program but should not preclude the teaching of an adequate program. Even in rooms where classroom furniture is stationary, a well-balanced program of physical education is quite possible. Table 6 on the following pages includes many kinds of play apparatus recommended for use in the elementary schools.

The Use of the Classroom. The teaching of physical education activities is facilitated by the availability of adequate space and suitable facilities. It is, however, entirely possible to plan and teach satisfactory programs even in situations where space and facilities are extremely limited. In a classroom where stationary furniture is used, activities may be adapted to the space in the front of the room or to the aisles between the desks and chairs. Many games, relay races, stunts, and rhythmic activities may be enjoyed with such an arrangement. It is quite possible to teach certain folk dances and singing games with the class arranged in a circle around the room, outside the rows of desks and chairs. Basic dance steps may be taught with children moving up and down the aisles. Square dances may at least be demonstrated by one set in the space at the front of the room. Small-group games may be enjoyed with groups organized in the corners of the room.

If the classroom is used as a play area, all safety precautions should be observed. Uncontrolled running about in a room where the furniture is permanently fixed is dangerous and should be avoided. Many activities, however, may be safely taught in the classroom and may be very enjoyable and worthwhile.

Table 6. Play Apparatus Recommended for Use in Elementary Schools

Equipment	Initial cost	Upkeep	Accident toll	Supervision required	Space for child served	Use to the child
Adjustable ladder	A	L	L	A	L	Provides for development of arms and shoulders. Good for stretching activity.
Balance beams	L	L	L	L	L	Good for developing the extensor muscles, particularly the lateral groups.
Basic block units	L	A	L	L	A	Provides for the imaginative play of young children.
Buck, or vaulting, box. .	H	L	L	A	L	Good for climbing over, jumping, and vaulting. Develops arms and shoulder-girdle muscles and a sense of timing.
Horizontal ladder	A	L	L	L	L	Excellent for stretching and for developing flexibility of arms and shoulder-girdle muscles.
Jungle-gym	H	L	L	L	L	Provides for general muscle development through hanging, climbing, and hand swinging.
Mats	A	A	L	L	L	Excellent for development of flexibility.

KEY:
A—Average
H—High
L—Low

Table 6. Play Apparatus Recommended for Use in Elementary Schools (continued)

Equipment	Initial cost	Upkeep	Accident toll	Supervision required	Space for child served	Use to the child
Rigid ladder and board.	L	A	L	A	L	Provides for general body development through climbing, hanging, balancing, and adjusting board.
Sand box	L	L	L	A	A	Provides opportunity for creative play.
Sewer tile	L	L	L	L	L	Good for developing trunk, legs, and shoulder muscles.
Slide	H	L	L	L	L	Develops courage in the young child.
Stall bars	H	L	L	L	L	Develops arm, shoulder, trunk, and leg muscles, through climbing and hanging.
Stilts	L	L	A	A	L	Excellent for developing balance, courage.
Swings	H	H	H	H	H	Provides pleasurable rather than developmental activity.
Turning poles or horizontal bar	L	L	L	A	L	Excellent for developing arms, shoulders, trunk, and general flexibility.

KEY:
A—Average
H—High
L—Low

45

Fundamental Group Formations. Organized activities in physical education, such as large-group games and dances, may be done in a variety of formations. The directions for some activities indicate a definite formation, while others permit a choice. In order that all types of activity may be enjoyed with the least possible confusion about group organization and formation, it is essential that children of elementary-school age be taught the formations most frequently used. It is also important that children learn how to take their positions in these formations quickly and without disorder. Figures 3–1 to 3–5 illustrate a number of the most commonly used group formations.

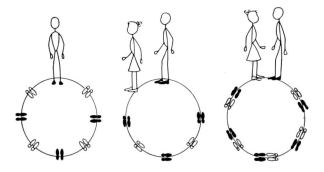

Figure 3–1. Single-circle Formation.
a. Single circle, facing center
b. Facing counterclockwise
c. Facing partners

Figure 3–2. Double-circle Formations: facing center.

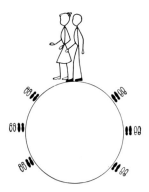

Figure 3–3. Double-circle Formations: facing counterclockwise.

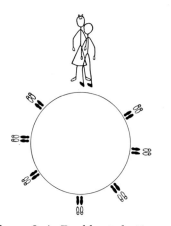

Figure 3–4. Double-circle Formations: facing partner.

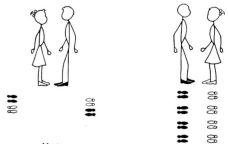

Figure 3–5. Line Formations.

SUMMARY

This chapter explains the value of a well-planned physical education program to ensure a balanced variety of activities. It stresses the importance of flexibility in program planning, so that the changing needs and interests of children may be met. Changing classroom situations, weather conditions, current problems, and interests are all considered. This chapter also indicates the important steps in planning a physical education lesson or unit of instruction. These steps are analyzed in a general way since planning, teaching, and learning involve certain factors common to all age groups or levels.

Chapter 4 deals with more definite methods and materials which may be used to accelerate and enrich learning in the physical education program of activities.

QUESTIONS AND PROBLEMS FOR DISCUSSION

1. What are three important steps in planning and teaching any activity?

2. Enumerate ways in which a teacher may economically budget the time allotted to physical education.

3. What determines the advisability of including physical education in a unit of instruction where another subject-matter area is the core?

4. Explain the values of both long-range and short-range planning.

SUGGESTED ACTIVITY UNIT

Plan a unit in which physical education is the core. The topic for study may be May Day. The origin and traditional practices cf May Day may be studied, traditional May Day dances may be learned, and the culmination may be a class or school May Day.

4. Enriching the Learning Process

In order that the objectives of physical education may be accomplished more readily, all methods and materials which facilitate the learning process should be explored. It is easy to fall into the path of least resistance, utilizing the same methods year after year and assuming that effective learning takes place.

Learning Is Complex. It is through the sensory mechanisms that understandings and meaningful concepts are acquired. Motivation and experiences and associations which vary from one person to another influence the learning pattern. The individual learns as a whole—specific facts must be acquired, attitudes formed, and skills mastered if total learning is to evolve. It becomes apparent that the psychology of learning must be recognized and its principles applied if teaching is to be effective.

The use of any materials and methods to accelerate learning may be justified, provided that they are educationally sound. Learning may extend from the one extreme of firsthand experience, in which the learner is directly involved, to the other extreme of oral instruction, in which what is spoken determines the kind of learning that takes place. Between these two extremes, audio-visual materials serve as an aid in the learning process.

LEARNING IN PHYSICAL EDUCATION

Children learn by:

1. Observing activities, experiments, films, filmstrips, slides, charts, graphs, pictures, etc.

2. Imitating skills thus observed

3. Listening to teacher, radio, phonograph records, sound films, tape recordings, etc.

4. Following directions

5. Practicing skills learned through any of the preceding media

6. Constructing workboards, flannelgraphs, puppets, etc. for game layouts and maneuvers

7. Sharing interviews, reports, films, filmstrips, dramatizations, exhibits

8. Reading and writing to obtain information; to express ideas; to distinguish between fact and opinion and between truth and superstition; to have fun; to develop interests and abilities

9. Creating through dramatizations, drawings, games, dances, etc.

10. Touring within the school, to other schools, to playgrounds, to parks, and to other places for competitive games and meets

A combination of three methods is effective in enriching the learning process in physical education: demonstration, explanation, and experience.

Demonstration

Chapter 3 suggested the importance of demonstration. Although everyone "learns to do by doing," the skills involved in achieving the objectives of physical education require careful teaching before the learner can obtain satisfaction in "doing." The correct way to throw, catch, or bat a ball, to climb a rope, to do a dance step, and to do many of the conditioning exercises are only a few of the skills which require demonstration as well as explanation in order to obtain most effective results. Demonstration may be given by the teacher, by a child who has learned the correct techniques, and/or through audio-visual aids. The teacher or the person who demonstrates should be certain of all steps in the skill before he attempts to give a demonstration.

Some of the principles that should guide the teacher in planning a demonstration are the following:

1. Preplan and rehearse the demonstration.

2. To maintain continuity, outline the steps as the lesson proceeds.

3. Repeat the steps as the lesson develops.

4. Summarize by repeating the entire demonstration.

5. Strive for simplicity.

6. Be sure the demonstration is visible to all.

7. Watch for the reactions of observers.
8. Do not *rush* the demonstration *or* make it too long.
9. Evaluate.

After observing and imitating the techniques of a skill well-demonstrated, a child may practice and become efficient in applying this skill in various situations.

Explanation

The method of explanation is most effectively used in situations where there is to be an application of skills already learned, but it is also used coincidentally with the demonstration method. Explanation and demonstration by the teacher, followed by performance and practice of the skill by each child, are more effective than explanation alone. However, a combination of demonstration and explanation supplemented by audio-visual materials ensures a process of learning which serves as a background for subsequent creative learnings and enriched experiences.

Direct Experiences

As noted previously, the most concrete and meaningful kind of experience is the one in which the individual is directly involved. A child does not learn to swim by watching others swim and never participating himself. The nature of physical education demands that the learner be an active participant if he is to acquire skills and put them into practice in a game situation. In order to develop big-muscle groups, activities such as running, climbing, jumping, kicking, and responding to rhythm, must be actually performed. However, if the child is to learn to do these activities skillfully, certain techniques may be effectively utilized to promote learning. It will be apparent, as the various audio-visual materials are discussed, that their use is determined by the type of activity being performed, the level of the age group, and the degree to which they satisfy the fulfillment of objectives. In the final analysis true learning in physical education results from the doing.

Contrived Experiences

The use of models and objects in contriving an experience in physical education presents innumerable possibilities. In presenting a new team game the teacher should actually show the pupils the equipment required—whether it be balls, racquets, or bats. By displaying these objects the teacher enables the children to form accurate concepts as to size, shape, and weight. These concepts help them make accurate associations when the teacher refers to a particular piece of equipment.

A model differs from the object in that it is a three-dimensional replica of the original, scaled up or down. Models of playing fields and courts can be useful aids in learning game rules and strategy. Whereas it may be difficult to teach positions, boundary lines, and court areas in the regulation situation, these learnings may be more easily acquired through the use of miniatures. Models of playing fields can be constructed by children and correlated with arithmetic as the children learn to scale to accurate proportions. Figures of players can be made from pipestem cleaners or colored pins. Magnetic boards of playing fields made of sheet metal, with tiny magnets attached to the objects representing the players, are another ingenious aid.

The use of models in conjunction with the safety lesson offers many possibilities, because sometimes it is not feasible to teach a safety lesson through a direct experience. Posture models may be constructed inexpensively or purchased commercially. Dolls in costume representing various countries serve as attractive aids to the dance program.

A word of caution is important at this point. The teacher must be alert to see that the learnings with the use of models are transferred to real situations; otherwise their use cannot be justified. Since models are often enlarged many times their actual size or cut down to a fraction of their true size, the learner may become confused in associating them with the realities for which they stand. The wise teacher knows when the devices described as contrived experiences can best aid in the learning process and uses them accordingly.

AUDIO-VISUAL AIDS

The wide use of audio-visual materials by the Armed Forces during World War II, the favorable results achieved in schoolrooms during the past decades, and research on retention of learning through audio-visual education signify the value of these aids. Some values of audio-visual materials are:

1. Creating interest and motivation
2. Providing a common denominator of experience
3. Making factors of time, space, and distance relatively insignificant
4. Widening the scope of learning and attention
5. Increasing retention

Motion Pictures

Motion pictures are probably the most commonly used of the audio-visual materials. Because they are so readily accepted they are often not used to the best advantage. "To show a movie" seems a simple enough procedure, but to present a film with preplanning, careful selection, and knowledge that it offers the best potential for learning in the specific situation is an approach that requires time and thought on the part of the teacher.

Films may be used to *introduce* a new activity and *arouse* interest; to *supplement* the verbal presentation and demonstration; or to *review* and *summarize* the skills learned.

The number of motion pictures available which present teaching of skills by the part method is limited. Usually the emphasis is upon the performance of the activity as a whole with reference to the skills only as they appear in the game situation.

In selecting films the following four criteria should be kept in mind: [1]

1. A useful film contains authoritative information.
2. A useful teaching film is keyed to a definite age group.
3. A useful teaching film must contribute to the group learning situation.
4. A useful teaching film is keyed to the curriculum problem or unit of study.

There have been experimental studies which reveal some of the values of motion pictures. The increased rate of learning, greater length of retention, and development of pupil interest are three of the most significant values.

The three steps in effective and skillful use of teaching films are

[1] Walter Arno Wittich and Charles Francis Schuller, *Audio-Visual Materials*, New York, Harper & Brothers, 1953, pp. 351–393.

preparation and preview, presentation under best possible conditions, and follow-up. The best possible film can become ineffective as a teaching aid if attention is not given to factors such as room darkening, acoustics, ventilation, setup of equipment in advance, seating, and other details concerned with actual projection.

Kinds of Motion Pictures. Motion-picture film may be classified as to size and content.

Film is of three sizes: 35-mm., theatrical film; 16-mm., educational film for school and community; and 8-mm., the home-movie type.[2]

Educational film may be either silent or sound. The latter is more widely used, but silent film has some excellent uses in physical education, where the commentary of the local teacher may be preferable to a prepared script. Films are obtainable in color or in black and white.

Motion pictures may be categorized into the following areas as to their function: [3]

1. Informational films inform, instruct, or provide knowledge or facts about people, processes, natural events, social conditions, past events, occupations, and theories.

2. Skill or drill films show how certain things are done in order to attain greatest speed, form, cleverness, and understanding.

3. Appreciation films develop wholesome, correct attitudes toward man, animals, things, or ideas.

4. Documentary films, or "idea films" show real people in real life situations.

5. Recreational films amuse or entertain.

6. Dramatic and episodic films are excerpts or episodes of varying length from feature films.

7. Cartoon films utilize cartoon, or animated diagrams to depict a process.

8. News films present current events.

9. Scientific films provide better understanding and supply factual information.

10. Industrial and sponsored films are all subsidized films made by special-interest groups.

[2] Mm. (millimeters) refers to width of film; 25 mm. equals 1 inch.
[3] Wittich and Schuller, *op. cit.*, pp. 216–228.

11. Provocative films are chiefly for discussion purposes with film forums and councils.

Newer Trends. Some of the comparatively new adaptations with motion-picture film should be mentioned, as they pertain to the area of physical education.

Loopfilms are free of certain limitations of other types of motion-picture film in teaching specific skills. Loopfilms are one continuous length of silent motion-picture film, between 5 and 20 feet, spliced together to form a loop. The repetitious element of the loopfilm is especially suitable for the presentation of a basic skill. In some types of activity it is even possible to view the loopfilm on a daylight screen while performing the skill simultaneously. A special attachment, which may be adapted to any type of projector, is necessary for the use of loopfilms.

Slow-motion photography and devices on projectors which allow for reversal or stoppage of the film are also valuable to the physical educator.

The 16-mm. magnetic-recording projector offers many possibilities for physical education departments that wish to take their own movies and record a script of their choice.

General Sources for Films. Films may be purchased, leased, rented, or borrowed without charge. The wide variety of sources can be confusing to a teacher who is just beginning to explore the field of motion pictures. Some of the most widely known film reference books are the following:

1. Krahn, Frederic A., ed., *Educational Film Guide.* New York: The H. W. Wilson Company. A comprehensive reference book of all 16-mm. motion pictures, published annually and brought up to date with quarterly supplements during the year. It is arranged according to title and subject index, classified subject list (using Dewey Decimal classification), and directory of main sources.

2. *Educators' Guide to Free Films.* Randolph, Wisc.: Educators' Progress Service. Published annually. Thirteen annual editions, 1953, contains 2,574 titles of free films.

3. *Blue Book of 16-mm. Films.* Chicago: Educational Screen, Inc. Contains 7,500 film titles indexed alphabetically and by subject; also an index to television sources, 1953.

4. *Evaluation Film Project.* New York: Educational Film Library Association. An extensive evaluation service, which is mailed out periodically to subscribers. Visual education specialists evaluate and annotate films.

5. State film libraries, usually connected with state educational departments or state universities.

6. State and local health departments.

7. Local education departments and public libraries.

8. Voluntary health agencies.

Specific Sources for Health, Physical Education, and Safety-film Listings

1. *Athletics and Physical Education in Film.* Chicago: Audio-Visual Publications, Inc., 1950.

2. *Audio-Visual Resources in Health and Welfare.* (Sponsored by *See and Hear.*) Chicago: Audio-Visual Publications, Inc., 1952.

3. Bernhard, Frederica, *Education Films in Sports.* New York: Educational Film Library Association, 1945.

4. "Checklist of 16-mm. Films for Primary Grades," *See and Hear,* 5 (4):27–32, December, 1949.

5. "Guide to Audio-Visual Resources for Sports and Physical Education," *See and Hear,* 5 (3):25–46, November, 1949.

6. Heimers, Lili, *Health Education for All Ages.* Montclair, N. J.: State Teachers College, 1944.

7. *National Directory of Safety Films.* Chicago: National Safety Council. Published annually.

8. *Sports, Physical Education, and Recreation Film Guide.* Chicago: Business Screen Magazine, 1947–1948.

9. *Sports Film Guide: Physical Education and Recreation Motion Pictures and Filmstrips.* Chicago: The Athletic Institute, 1952.

10. *Sports Teaching Aids: Audio-Visual,* card catalogue. Washington: NSWA, 1951.

Radio—Recordings

The recognition of radio and recordings as educational materials brought about a change in the terminology of the "visual education" field. A broader concept became necessary to identify the supplementary aids, which now utilized the auditory sense as well as the visual.

Radio may be utilized from two different approaches in education—in one, the child is a passive listener to a program selected for its possible contributions to the curriculum; in the other, the child actively participates in a radio broadcast over the local station or the school-owned station.

Immediacy and reality, as well as emotional impact and group values, are some of the specific advantages of radio.

Programs with make-believe characters, nursery rhymes, or folk tunes appeal to young children. The application of radio to elementary physical education does not offer too many possibilities, although sometimes this technique of audio education may be very valuable.

Many state departments of education have become conscious of the need to make available to schools audio materials of instruction. Tape libraries are rapidly increasing as a function of these departments, and one of the services which they provide is the duplication from a master tape for the school's permanent collection. The Federal Radio Education Committee, in cooperation with the Office of Education, publishes a catalogue of *Radio Recordings: A Transcription Service to Schools.*

Phonograph records have been successfully used in elementary physical education, especially in the rhythmic program. Disk and tape recordings now make it possible to re-record special radio programs, concerts, and individual performances to be utilized as each situation requires. Custom-made recordings of special music, which can be individualized by reference to members of the class, captivate the interest of young children.

Methods by which radio and recordings can supplement classroom teachings vary from one situation to another. It is up to the teacher to determine whether or not the results of radio and recordings justify their use as educational techniques.

Stills

Filmstrips. Many of the same principles which apply to the use of motion-picture films are equally applicable to the filmstrip. This is a technique which has expanded in its usefulness as a teaching tool and is becoming increasingly advantageous in the area of physical education.

The filmstrip is a series of frames printed on 35-mm. motion-picture film. There are anywhere from ten to a hundred frames or pictures in a single filmstrip. Flexibility, compactness, inexpensiveness, simplicity, continuity, and unbreakableness, as well as ease of projection and storage, make it a popular teaching material. In situations where it is not necessary that motion be depicted, the filmstrip can serve a useful purpose. A picture may be retained for discussion and prolonged viewing. Many motion pictures are now available with accompanying filmstrips, which are used for review and clarification. The filmstrip may be black and white or color, and it may be silent or sound. In the silent version, captions appear beneath the frame or prepared script is provided. The sound filmstrip has a synchronized recording on which a signal warns the projectionist when to change to the next frame.

Projectors for filmstrips usually have an attachment incorporated for the showing of 35-mm. or 2″ by 2″ slides. "Beginning skill" sound filmstrips are appearing in increasing numbers in the various sports activities in physical education. To date, only a limited number is available for the elementary level, specifically, but there is indication that they will eventually be produced on a large scale. Some sources of filmstrips are the following:

1. *Filmstrip Guide.* New York: The H. W. Wilson Company. A cumulative classified index published quarterly.

2. *The Complete Index of Educational Filmstrips.* Madison, Wisc.: Filmstrip Distributors. Classified according to subject, grade level, and units of application. Represents sixty-one major commercial producers.

3. *Educators Guide to Free Slidefilms.* Randolph, Wisc.: Educators' Progress Service. Published annually.

4. Falconer, Vera M., *Filmstrips: A Descriptive Index and Users' Guide.* New York: McGraw-Hill Book Company, Inc.

5. *Sports Film Guide: Filmstrips in Physical Education and Recreation.* Chicago: The Athletic Institute.

Slides. Slides may be of two common sizes—2″ by 2″, miniature, and 3¼″ by 4″, standard or lantern. They may be photographic or handmade. The latter type is made of cellophane, typed materials, pencil, crayon, or colored ink on etched glass, silhouettes, India ink, or ceramics. Here is an audio-visual medium which affords an opportunity for even the primary-grade children to display creativeness and self-expression.

Many of the qualities of the filmstrip apply to slides, the basic difference being that the latter do not have to be shown in any particular order. The specific slides which aid in achieving a purpose may be selected.

Kinder enumerates the following criteria for evaluating slides: [4]

1. Authenticity
2. Simplicity
3. Relative size of items
4. Photography
5. Artistry
6. Mechanical quality

The use of slides in diagramming plays in team sports, portraying safety lessons, or conveying health messages should be considered by classroom teachers. Slides can be substituted for posters as a means of expressing certain ideas, and the results of pupils' work can be projected on the screen with slides.

Opaque Projection. The opaque projector offers the means by which graphic, nontransparent materials may be projected on the screen. Materials up to 8½ by 11 inches in size—small objects, specimens, selections from textbooks—may be viewed through the projector.

In physical education, diagrams of team games, dance-step patterns or formations, and pictures of native costumes may be projected directly from the source for all to view simultaneously. Health and safety materials are easily adapted to opaque projection. Instead of the usual single picture a series of pictures may be pasted on a long strip of wrapping paper for insertion into the projector. An outline of a physical education activity may be projected on a chalk-covered blackboard instead of the traditional screen, and children asked to fill in certain areas in order to complete the desired effect. A small poster may be enlarged

[4] James S. Kinder, *Audio-Visual Materials and Techniques*, New York, American Book Company, 1950, pp. 170–171.

many times by projection onto a large sheet of white cardboard, and since it will be magnified many times, tracing the outline will be simple. "If there is a limit to suggestions for the opaque projector, it is the limit of the imagination and versatility of the teacher." [5]

Symbolic Representations

Visual Symbols. Although these symbolic representations often are not considered audio-visual materials, it would be difficult to conceive of a classroom where they are not commonly used. Included under this classification are eight types of graphic material which are representations of reality. They are cartoons, diagrams, posters, flat maps, graphs, comic strips, charts, and drawings or sketches. Their value lies chiefly in their power to attract attention and to present ideas in a brief and condensed form. The use of these teaching materials is not new to the classroom teacher. The *blackboard,* or, in more current terminology, the chalkboard, is a familiar sight in schools. Likewise, the *bulletin board,* or tackboard, has been used to present various kinds of material in visualized form. It is the medium for displaying the graphic materials mentioned above. The particular value of this device lies in the opportunity it offers for pupil planning and creativeness. Three-dimensional effects may be achieved to represent equipment, and pipe cleaners may be bent in appropriate shapes to portray the various activities. Bright and contrasting colors help to make outstanding displays.

The physical education program offers a wide range of uses for *charts, graphs,* and *diagrams.* Group and individual accomplishments in self-testing activities may be recorded for pupil interest. Weight and height graphs are a common example of this type of visual symbol; line graphs, bar graphs, pie charts, area graphs, or pictorial graphs are additional types that can be utilized. It would be difficult to conceive of team games being introduced without some diagrammatic sketch to clarify rules or indicate game strategy.

Behavior, especially that of younger children, can often be influenced through messages conveyed by artistic *posters.* A simple

[5] *Ibid.,* p. 181.

idea expressed by a poster may have greater impact than the verbal admonitions of the teacher in reminding pupils of rules of conduct, sportsmanship, personal hygiene, and respect for property. Scientific use of color has become an important factor in poster construction. Poster making is popular in modern schools.

There is a limited use for *cartoons* on the elementary level; since they are abstract interpretations of ideas or points of view, they are better adapted to more mature individuals. *Comic books,* which have gained extensive popularity as sources of entertainment for youth, are emerging with some educational contributions that heretofore have not been recognized. Their use in physical education has been restricted to the "hero-worship" type which aims to influence young children to practice health habits endorsed by some well-known athletic figure.

One of the newer display techniques is the *feltboard,* or flannelgraph, which operates on the principle that these materials will adhere to like surfaces. The felt or flannel is stretched over a wooden, masonite, or heavy surface. Letters, words, numbers, and other cutouts made of identical material will adhere. Models of game situations on playing fields are an example of the use of this type of device.

Although *maps* have relatively little use in elementary physical education, the identification of a country on a map can serve to make the learning of a folk dance more meaningful. *Flat pictures* are substitutes for reality and can faithfully reproduce actual situations. Posture pictures can help children to note any departures from normal posture positions.

The alert teacher explores all potentialities which these graphic materials offer and encourages student participation in preparing them for use in particular teaching situations.

Verbal Symbols. It would be almost an impossibility to teach without the use of words to convey ideas and information. Despite Edison's prediction that the motion picture would replace the printed word, even the most progressive educator undoubtedly agrees that textbooks are here to stay. Symbols or words stand for experiences. It is the job of the teacher to offer sufficient kinds of meaningful experiences so that pupils can associate ideas, words, principles, and abstractions with experiences already acquired.

Even though physical education connotes activity, it is important that rules of the game, descriptions of activities, and names of equipment and apparatus be available on the printed page. It is apparent that abstract learnings depend on experiences for proper interpretation and that concrete experiences require verbal symbols so that the learner can properly refer to the experience when it no longer exists.

Television

Undoubtedly the most challenging of the educational media today is television. Experimentation is being carried on to explore the educational potential of this dynamic tool for learning. Television adds the visual to radio and consequently compels full attention of the audience. It enables man to bring the sound of radio and the action of motion pictures to the audience; moreover, events can be broadcast as they take place.

Although education in general may utilize television for programs of interest which may enrich the curriculum, one of the greatest contributions which TV can make to physical education in particular is in the realm of public relations. A program emanating from an actual class situation brings the children and their performances into the home. Teaching of skills by an expert or a nationally famous figure is another example of television's contribution to physical education. Athletic contests were among the first type of program to be televised, since they offer a great source of entertainment and interest to the public. There is the possibility that a great majority of schools will have transmitting stations of their own. However, closed-circuit television, which brings buildings and rooms together through coaxial cable, is a type of facility which holds great promise, for the program can be channeled anywhere in the system and is wholly the responsibility of the school.

Television must achieve certain standards in order to qualify as a useful teaching tool. The program televised should: [6]
1. Have an educational purpose
2. Provide the possibility of continuity

[6] Harold E. Wigren, "What Is an Educational TV Program?" *Educational Screen*, December, 1952, pp. 420–422, 435–437.

3. Present an educational philosophy consistent with democratic values

4. Be based upon the needs and problems of the viewers

5. Serve as a means of growth and development for the individual who views it

6. Involve the viewer as a participant

7. Be a means of bringing many creative and thought-provoking experiences to individuals

8. Be presented in an atmosphere of objectivity

9. Be flexible in its design and approach

10. Communicate clearly and effectively

Creative and Shared Experiences

Dramatizations. At the elementary level, children may participate in creative dramatics in which they act out some experiences and develop their own action and commentary. This is usually the result of meaningful group planning, emphasizing the benefits which accrue rather than stressing the finished product with costumes, lighting, and staging. Mother Goose rhymes, poems, experiences from reality, folk tales, legends, and the lives of historical characters provide material that is easily dramatized by the child. The values of creative dramatics are described as stimulation of social development, development of creative self-expression, wholesome emotional development, development of fine attitudes and appreciations, and development of inner security. Creative dramatics through simple rhythmic movements are a challenge to elementary-school children. Other forms of dramatics which have limited application on the elementary level in physical education are the pageant, the tableau, and the puppet show.

Excursions. Advantages of field trips are limited in the area of physical education. There are, however, many opportunities in health and safety teaching for this audio-visual experience which takes the students outside the regular classroom. A teacher may take a group of children to another room or to another school to observe the performance of a group in some physical activity. This experience is valuable for observers and performers alike. The performing group may invite the observers to participate in the activity and thus add to the enjoyment of both groups.

Sharing Exhibits. "An exhibit is an arrangement of realistic materials which is designed to inform the observer about a subject of educational significance." [7] The objects and models described previously may be used in the display or exhibit to explain the scope and content of a physical education program. The exhibit can serve not only as a means of sharing information but also as a medium for public relations. Planning and the use of artistic techniques of color, design, and simplicity are essential to the preparation of an exhibit.

GUIDES IN THE USE OF AUDIO-VISUAL MATERIALS

The following general principles should be clearly understood and followed as guides in the use of audio-visual materials:

1. Audio-visual materials require careful preparation and planning for effective utilization.

2. No one aid is better than another; the value of each depends upon the purpose for which it is being used.

3. Audio-visual materials are not intended as substitutes for formal teaching; they should be regarded as supplementary techniques.

4. Students should not remain passive participants but must be involved actively with responsibility for what is taking place.

5. Materials should be examined for scientific accuracy.

6. Continuous evaluation of the results achieved with audio-visual materials is important for future planning.

SUMMARY

Education is more satisfactory if a variety of methods, techniques, and materials is utilized. Learning is complex. Understandings and meaningful concepts are acquired not only through reading and writing but also through the sensory mechanisms, through experiences and associations, through listening, observing, collecting, creating, sharing, and constructing.

Audio-visual materials are extremely valuable in many situations. They create interest, provide profitable experiences, widen the scope of learning, and eliminate many problems of time, space, and distance.

[7] Wittich and Schuller, *op. cit.*, p. 221.

The importance of using a combination of methods in teaching has been emphasized in this chapter. The methods described here in general terms should be applied as needed in following the directions and interpreting the descriptions of the specific activities for the different age levels designated in the next four chapters. Chapter 5 indicates the characteristics and needs of five- and six-year-old children and it describes the games, stunts, dances, and rhythmic activities which help to meet these needs.

QUESTIONS AND TOPICS FOR DISCUSSION

1. How do children learn?
2. What are three methods of teaching that enrich the learning process in physical education?
3. What are the principles that should guide a teacher in planning a demonstration lesson?
4. When is the method of explanation most effectively used?
5. Why and how does the use of audio-visual materials facilitate learning?
6. What are the various types of audio-visual materials most suitable for use with children of elementary-school age?
7. How do audio-visual materials make a unique contribution to the physical education program?
8. What are some of the principles which should govern the use of audio-visual materials?

SUGGESTED PROBLEM

Prepare an annotated bibliography or source list of materials that may be used to enrich the teaching of one of the units developed in Chapters 1, 2, or 3.

ADDITIONAL QUESTIONS AND TOPICS FOR DISCUSSION— PART ONE

1. What are the broad objectives of the total school program?
2. Compare the strengths and weaknesses in the procedures followed by the successful progressive teacher and the successful traditional teacher.

3. How does physical education provide for enrichment of experience, and how does it contribute to the total school program?

4. What should the teacher consider before he correlates and/or integrates physical education with a unit of instruction?

5. Why should physical education in the elementary school retain its identity as a major area of learning?

6. How are the depth and scope of educational learnings enhanced through the use of stories such as "Josie's Home Run"?

7. Discuss in detail the elements of a good lesson plan.

8. What other factors contribute to the teaching of a skill or activity?

9. Describe some well-balanced weekly programs of physical education for the lower grades and for the upper grades.

10. Discuss the various types of play apparatus, their use, the supervision needed for them, and their value in satisfying the physical needs of elementary-school children.

11. How does a well-organized program of physical education influence individual pupil behavior and relationships among pupils?

SUGGESTED REFERENCES—PART ONE

BOOKS

Caswell, H. L., and A. W. Foshey, *Education in the Elementary School.* New York: American Book Company, 1950.

Chandler, Anna, and Irene Cypher, *Audio-Visual Techniques.* New York: Noble and Noble, Publishers, Inc., 1948.

Children in Focus. Washington: American Association for Health, Physical Education, and Recreation, 1954.

Cowell, C. C., and H. W. Hazelton, *Curriculum Designs in Physical Education.* Englewood Cliffs, N. J.: Prentice-Hall, Inc., 1955.

Dale, Edgar, *Audio-Visual Methods in Teaching.* New York: The Dryden Press, 1946.

Dent, E. C., *Audio-Visual Handbook.* Chicago: Society for Visual Education, 1949.

Department of Elementary School Principals, *Aids to Teaching in the Elementary School.* Washington: National Education Association, Thirteenth Yearbook, 1934.

Hanna, Lavone, et al., *Unit Teaching in the Elementary Schools*. New York: Rinehart and Company, Inc., 1955.

Jones, E., E. Morgan, and G. Stevens, *Methods and Materials in Elementary Physical Education*. Yonkers, New York: World Book Company, 1950.

Kinder, James S., *Audio-Visual Materials and Techniques*. New York: American Book Company, 1950.

Knapp, W. L., and F. R. Todd, *Democratic Leadership in Physical Education*. Millbrae, Calif.: California National Press, 1952.

La Salle, D., *Physical Education for the Classroom Teacher*. New York: A. S. Barnes and Company, 1937.

McCluskey, F. D., *Audio-Visual Teaching Techniques*. Dubuque, Iowa: Wm. C. Brown Company, 1949.

O'Keefe, P., and H. Fahey, *Education through Physical Activities*. St. Louis: The C. V. Mosby Company, 1949.

Sehon, E., et al., *Rhythms in Elementary Education*. New York: A. S. Barnes and Company, 1951.

Vannier, M., and M. Foster, *Teaching Physical Education in Elementary Schools*. Philadelphia: W. B. Saunders Company, 1954.

Voltmer, E. F., and A. A. Esslinger, *The Organization and Administration of Physical Education*. New York: Appleton-Century-Crofts, Inc., 1949.

Williams, J. F., and C. L. Brownell, *The Administration and Organization of Health and Physical Education*. Philadelphia: W. B. Saunders Company, 1946.

PAMPHLETS

McNeely, S. A., and E. Schneider, *Physical Education in the School Child's Day*. Washington: U. S. Government Printing Office, 1950.

Physical Education for Children of Elementary-school Age. Chicago: The Athletic Institute, 1951.

Part Two

Developing the Program

5. Program for the Five- and Six-year-olds

This chapter considers five- and six-year-old children—their growth and development; their needs, capabilities, and interests; their behavior; and how a physical education program may be planned for them.

Growth and Development. Specialists in child growth and development agree that children of this age are passing through a period of slow but steady physical growth. There is good motor control of the large-muscle groups, but the smaller muscles are not yet well-developed. Most of these children have satisfactory speech habits. There is a tendency toward farsightedness, as the eyes are not yet mature. Right-handedness or left-handedness may have become apparent. The heart develops rapidly during this period of growth. These children are active and energetic, but they tire rather quickly and show plainly the signs of fatigue. The most common of these signs are inattention, restlessness, general lack of interest, and impatience.

Children at this age are learning to share, to take turns, and to consider others. They are becoming emotionally stable. They seek love and affection, praise and security. Although they enjoy doing things with others they are primarily individualistic.

Five- and six-year-olds are enthusiastic and eager to learn. They are curious and observant. Although their powers of concentration have been developed to some degree, their attention span remains short. An eye for detail and a strong liking for fantasy are both apparent. These children have a strong urge to dramatize, but at the same time they are beginning to evaluate themselves and their achievements.

The Needs of These Children. Because children in this group have the characteristics previously enumerated, they have certain needs that must be satisfied. They must have vigorous and varied physical exercise which involves the large-muscle groups. They need stimulating activities which arouse their curiosity and interest. They require frequent rest and relaxation periods. They should be given the opportunity to play in groups. They need, perhaps more than anything else, the sympathetic understanding of their teachers.

An Example of Effective Planning. One group of five- and six-year-old children became interested in cowboys and the "wild West." These children tore rampantly over the playground, shooting, lassoing, and shouting. They resembled a herd of cattle on stampede. They directed all their energy toward specific objectives—chasing, capturing, overpowering the enemy, and outshouting all other children on the playground. These little folks became overstimulated, overactive, and greatly fatigued. Their teacher realized the need for guiding this tremendous energy, drive, and vigor into more productive channels. She knew that the power of these active, fiery individuals should be utilized, but harnessed and wisely directed. She believed that their interest in cowboys, if constructively used, might serve as a stimulation for new and valuable learnings.

The teacher asked herself, "What program of activity might meet the physical, mental, social, and emotional needs of these children, challenge their abilities, and still make good use of their current interest in things Western?" The answer seemed to be the dramatization of a rodeo. So, into a rodeo they all galloped.

Great plans were soon in progress. The children, with the help of their teacher, decided that the activities of a rodeo included roping or lassoing, riding, breaking horses, throwing calves, singing around the campfire, playing guitars, and telling stories. They realized that they needed to learn more about these activities before they could dramatize them in their play. They found and read books about ranch life. They brought to school cowboy and cowgirl costumes, lariats, guitars, phonograph records of Western music, and even a motion picture about the West. The teacher worked carefully with the children, making sure that the resources available were used to the best advantage and that activities planned ensured optimum achievement and satisfaction.

Enjoying the Activities. Galloping on imaginary horses and swinging lassos in response to suitable musical rhythm provided vigorous exercise. Cowboy tunes sung around a make-believe campfire provided relaxation. The children made cigar-box and cardboard guitars and strummed them with all seriousness. And they planned a real culmination—a rodeo program to which they invited their parents. Because the unit of instruction was composed of many short, interesting activities, there was no difficulty in motivating or retaining the children's interest.

An Evaluation. The children in the rodeo group developed improved coordination and skill in using their arm and leg muscles. They enjoyed their relaxation periods. They acquired much information relating to cowboys, ranch life, and the West in general. They enriched their reading and spelling vocabularies. They gained valuable experience in oral and written expression. *And they had fun.*

Thus this unit, through the development of well-planned rhythmic and other physical activities, guided the interest and utilized the energies of a group of children who were in danger of being overstimulated and perhaps harmed by rough-and-tumble play. It opened doors to wider learnings, better understandings, and greater appreciation of the Western way of life. Best of all, these children shared their fun with their parents and with friends in other classes.

It is possible to plan and enjoy many types of units in which children's interests and the objectives of physical education for this age level coincide. Therefore, a teacher must be familiar with many games, stunts, rhythms, and dances that capture the interest of children at this level of growth and development.

The remainder of this chapter is devoted to descriptions of and suggestions for teaching a variety of activities suitable for the physical education program. The activities described by no means represent a complete program, but, rather, are typical examples of many varieties of games, stunts, rhythms, and dances in which children of five and six years may participate profitably. The Selected References beginning on page 219 provide many excellent sources of additional activities.

GAMES

Games that are adapted to the interests, needs, and abilities of this age group are necessarily very simple. Children five and six years old should be taught games in which they learn to catch, throw, and bounce balls. Games including such skills contribute to the development of muscular coordination, accuracy, and self-control. Games like Musical Chairs, Jack-in-the-box, and Bird Catcher help to develop habits of listening, following directions, and responding quickly and accurately to signals and directions.

Outdoor—Large-group Games

A. Airplanes
  1. *Purpose*
     a. To respond quickly to the starting signal
     b. To learn to play according to rules
     c. To learn to play fair
  2. *Equipment*
     None
  3. *Description*
     The class is divided into several groups of even size (not more than four in a group). Each group lines up behind a starting line, with the players in each group standing one behind the other. The first child in each group spreads his arms to represent airplane wings. On a signal, this first child runs to a base line about 10 yards from the starting line and returns, imitating an airplane all the way. When a second starting signal is given, the next child in each group runs, and so on until all have had a turn. The winner of each heat then competes against all other winners.

B. Animal Race
  1. *Purpose*
     a. To learn to follow directions
     b. To learn to respond quickly to a signal
     c. To learn to play fair
  2. *Equipment*
     None

3. *Description*

Children stand side by side, toeing a starting line. Another line is drawn about 10 yards from the starting line. The children select an animal they would like to imitate. When the starting signal is given, all the children assume a position typical of the animal chosen. They then race to the finish line, moving like the chosen animal. The winner selects the next animal to be imitated.

Caution: Teacher should instruct the children to await the signal and to avoid touching another animal; she should be sure that the finish line is not too near a wall or fence, because the hazard of children running into such an object is too great.

C. Brownies and Fairies

1. *Purpose*
   a. To learn to be alert
   b. To learn to play fair
   c. To learn to respond quickly to a signal
   d. To learn to run fast
   e. To learn to turn and run on signal

2. *Equipment*
   None

3. *Description*

Two parallel lines are drawn about 30 feet apart. The class is divided into two groups of even size: one group of fairies, one group of brownies. The fairies stand behind one line, the brownies behind the other. The fairies turn their backs to the brownies, while the brownies creep up behind them as quietly as possible. One fairy watches the brownies and, as they come near, calls out, "Here come the brownies." When this signal is given, the fairies turn and chase the brownies back to their own line. All brownies caught by fairies then become fairies. Next the brownies turn their backs while the fairies creep up behind them. This procedure goes on, with each group having the same number of turns, until the time for the game is used up. The group with the greater number of players wins.

D. Sunshine and Shadow

   1. *Purpose*

      a. To learn to follow directions

      b. To learn to dodge and run fast

      c. To learn to take a chance

      d. To learn how to tag

   2. *Equipment*

     None

   3. *Description*

     One child is the sun and stands in the sunshine. The other children stand in shady places within a definite area of the playground. Whenever a child ventures into the sunshine the sun may chase that child. Any child tagged by the sun changes places with the sun.

E. Back Ball

   1. *Purpose*

      a. To improve skill in throwing and catching

      b. To learn to be alert

   2. *Equipment*

     Two 8-inch rubber balls

   3. *Description*

     Children are divided into two groups of even size and arranged as in the diagram. Two children stand between the groups. Each of these children holds a ball.

```
O  O  O  O                X  X  X  X

O  O  O  O                X  X  X  X
              O      X
O  O  O  O                X  X  X  X

O  O  O  O                X  X  X  X
```

Each of the children in the center throws the ball backward over his head to his group. One point is scored if the ball is caught before it touches the ground. The child who catches the ball goes to the center and becomes the next tosser. If the ball is not caught, no score is made, and the tosser takes another turn. The group scoring the greater number of points wins.

F. Busy Bee

1. *Purpose*
   a. To learn to follow directions
   b. To learn to move quickly
2. *Equipment*
   None
3. *Description*
   Children stand in the playing area in couples; there is one extra player. The teacher calls out the directions "face to face" or "back to back," and the children do as the directions indicate. When the teacher calls out, "Busy bee," all change partners. The extra player tries to get a partner. The child who is left without a partner becomes the extra player the next time.

G. Roll Ball

1. *Purpose*
   a. To roll the ball accurately
   b. To keep the ball from rolling out of the circle
2. *Equipment*
   A 6-inch rubber ball
3. *Description*
   Children join hands in a circle with one child in the center. The child in the center rolls the ball, attempting to make it go out of the circle. The children in the circle try to prevent this by pushing the ball back into the circle with their hands. The child who lets the ball go out of the circle between his feet or on his right then goes into the center and tries to roll the ball out.

H. Squirrel in the Tree

1. *Purpose*
   a. To learn to respond to a signal
   b. To learn to move quickly
2. *Equipment*
   None
3. *Description*
   Children arrange themselves into groups of two, with

hands joined. Each group has in its center a child who is known as a squirrel. There is one squirrel who has no tree. When the teacher gives a signal all squirrels change trees. The squirrel without a tree tries to get one. The child who is left out is the odd squirrel the next time. After every few plays, those who are trees should become squirrels, and vice versa.

Children must remain in their trees until a signal is given and change trees when the signal is given. The penalty for moving without the signal is to lose the chance to be a squirrel.

I. Water Sprite
1. *Purpose*
   a. To learn to run fast and to dodge
   b. To learn to listen for a signal and to respond quickly
2. *Equipment*
   None
3. *Description*
   The class is divided into two groups of even size. Two parallel lines are drawn about 20 feet apart to represent a river. A group stands on either "bank," with players toeing the line. The groups face each other, and one child, known as the water sprite, stands in the middle of the river. The sprite beckons quietly to any child, who in turn beckons to any child in the other group. These two children attempt to change places with one another without being tagged by the water sprite. A child tagged becomes the sprite.

Outdoor—Small-group Games

A. Rope Jumping
1. *Purpose*
   a. To learn to jump rope doing different stunts
   b. To learn to jump according to rules
2. *Equipment*
   A jump rope 16 feet long
3. *Description*
   Two children turn the rope, while the others, in turn, do the following:

    a. Run in and through the rope without stopping
    b. Jump ten times without stopping
    c. Run in and through the rope with a partner
    d. Run in with a partner, jump five times, then run out
    e. Make up a stunt and do it.

B. Tag

1. *Purpose*
     a. To learn to run fast
     b. To learn to dodge
     c. To learn to avoid being tagged
2. *Equipment*
   None
3. *Description*
   The child who has been chosen to be "it" runs among the other members of the group trying to tag someone. Whoever is tagged becomes "it." Boundaries of play should be determined before the game is started.

C. Bounce the Ball

1. *Purpose*
     a. To learn to bounce a ball accurately
     b. To learn to take turns
     c. To learn to catch a ball
2. *Equipment*
   One 6-inch rubber ball for each group of children. There should be no more than ten children in a group.
3. *Description*
   The group of children form a circle, with one child standing in the center. The child in the center bounces the ball in turn to each member of the group. Each child, as soon as he receives the ball, bounces it back to the child in the center. When each child has had a turn, a new leader is chosen. The game continues until all children have been leaders.

D. Find Me

1. *Purpose*
     a. To learn to play fair
     b. To learn to throw a beanbag back over the head
2. *Equipment*
   One beanbag for each group of ten children

3. *Description*

Each group of children selects a leader who stands in front of the group, with his back turned to the other players. The leader tosses the beanbag back over his head, and when one member of the group catches it, all members of the group clasp their hands behind them and, in unison, call out, "Find me." The leader then turns around and makes one guess as to which player is holding the beanbag. If he guesses correctly, he keeps his place. If he guesses incorrectly, the child who is holding the beanbag becomes the leader.

E. **Three-player Dodge Ball**

1. *Purpose*
   a. To learn to dodge
   b. To learn to throw a beanbag
   c. To learn to catch a beanbag

2. *Equipment*

A beanbag for each group of three children

3. *Description*

The group of three children stand in a single line, with the two end children facing the one in the center. The

Figure 5–1. Three-player Dodge Ball

center child is the dodger. The two children on the ends of the line try to strike the center child with the beanbag. The one who succeeds in doing this becomes the dodger.

F. Toss and Bounce

1. *Purpose*

   To learn to throw, bounce, and catch a ball

2. *Equipment*

   A 6-inch rubber ball for each group of ten or twelve children

3. *Description*

   The group of ten or twelve children stand in a circle, all players facing the center. A leader, who stands in the center of the circle, tosses the ball to each player in the group. Each player bounces the ball back to the leader. When each child in the group has caught and bounced the ball, a new leader is chosen.

G. Ball Stand

1. *Purpose*

   a. To learn the skills of throwing and catching a ball

   b. To learn to respond quickly to a signal

2. *Equipment*

   A 6-inch rubber ball

3. *Description*

   The children stand outside a 6-foot circle which has been drawn on the ground. A ball is placed in the circle. The leader calls out the name of any child in the group. This child goes to the center of the circle to pick up the ball. All the other children run as far away from the circle as possible before the leader picks up the ball and shouts, "Stand!" When this signal is given, all children must stand wherever they are. The leader then throws the ball, attempting to strike any other child. If he succeeds, the child he strikes becomes the next leader. After the call "stand" is heard, the other children may dodge, but not move their feet.

Indoor—Large-group Games

A. Circle Stoop

1. *Purpose*

   a. To learn to react quickly

   b. To learn self-control

2. *Equipment*
None

3. *Description*
Children stand one behind the other in single-circle formation. At a given signal, the children march, run, or skip
around the room. When the teacher gives the next signal,
everyone stoops. The last child to stoop goes out of the
game. The child who remains longest in the game is the
winner.

The game may be played with music, with the teacher
starting the music for the first signal and stopping it for
the second. If the game is played without music a hand-
clap is suggested as an appropriate signal.

Fouls: It is a foul to stoop before the signal is given. The
penalty is elimination from the game. As children are
eliminated, they form a new circle and continue in the
game. The aim is to remain in the original circle.

B. **Musical Chairs**

1. *Purpose*
a. To learn to respond quickly to a signal
b. To learn to wait for a signal

2. *Equipment*
None

3. *Description*
Children march in single-circle formation around the room
or around a row of chairs. When the music stops, each
child tries to secure a chair in which to sit. There should
always be at least one more child than there are chairs.
Failure to secure a chair eliminates a child from the game.
The child who remains longest in the game wins.

Fouls: It is a foul to sit before the music stops. Penalty for
a foul is elimination from the game. Upon elimination, children become members of a new group.

C. **Jack-in-the-box**

1. *Purpose*
a. To learn to respond quickly to a signal
b. To learn to wait for a signal

2. *Equipment*
None

3. *Description*
Children stand in an informal group. When the teacher says, "Jack-in-the-box!" everyone stoops. When the teacher says, "Jack-out-of-the-box!" everyone jumps to a standing position. The last child to respond each time is eliminated from the game. The child who remains longest in the game wins. New groups are formed by those eliminated.

D. Magic Carpet

1. *Purpose*
   a. To develop alertness
   b. To avoid being caught standing on the carpet when the music stops

2. *Equipment*
None

3. *Description*
Spaces about 3 feet square are marked off on the floor. These spaces are the magic carpets and are so arranged around the room that as the children march in a circle they must walk across them. Whenever the music stops, all marching ceases at once. Those children who are then standing on the carpets are eliminated from the game. The game continues until all but one child are eliminated. New carpets are marked off for use by those eliminated.

E. Rainbow

1. *Purpose*
   a. To improve skill in throwing and catching a beanbag or a ball
   b. To learn to respond quickly to a signal

2. *Equipment*
A 6-inch rubber ball or a beanbag

3. *Description*
Children are arranged in several groups of even size. The groups are arranged in rows, with the children in each row standing in single file, all facing the teacher. The rows are arranged side by side. Each row is given a color name. The teacher calls out a color name and throws the ball

or beanbag to the first child in that row; the child catches it and runs around to the rear position in his row. All other children in the row move forward a step. The teacher continues to call color names, making sure that each row re-receives an equal number of calls. Whenever a child fails to catch the ball or beanbag, he is eliminated from the game. The row with the greatest number of players left when time is called wins the game. Those eliminated retire to another part of the room for practice in responding.

Indoor—Small-group Games

A. Beanbag in the Circle

1. *Purpose*
   a. To learn to take turns
   b. To learn to play fair
   c. To learn accuracy in aiming and throwing
2. *Equipment*
   Four beanbags
3. *Description* (see Figure 5–2)
   Two concentric circles are drawn on the floor. The outside circle is about 30 inches in diameter, the inside circle about 18 inches. A group of six or eight children line up, one behind the other, about 8 feet from the circles. Each child in the group, in turn, tosses the beanbags, one at a time, into the circles. Beanbags which drop into the outer circle score the player 1 point, and those which drop into the inner circle score 2 points.

   Caution: Children should be instructed to keep one foot on the throwing line and to stay out of the way of the thrower.

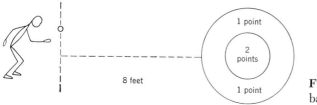

Figure 5–2. Bean-bag in the Circle

B. Schoolroom Bowling
1. *Purpose*
   a. To develop accuracy in aiming at a target and rolling a ball
   b. To learn to knock down bowling pins at a distance of 10 feet
2. *Equipment*
   Bowling pins and balls (Indian clubs, blackboard erasers, or oblong blocks will serve as substitutes for regular pins; 6-inch rubber balls, sponge-rubber balls, or tennis balls may be used.)
3. *Description*
   The bowling pins are set up in regular formation, at a distance of 8 inches from each other. A group of not more than eight children stand in single file behind a starting line, at a distance of 10 feet from the pins. Each child in turn rolls one ball, attempting to knock down the pins. One point is scored for each pin knocked down. The child scoring highest wins. Each child serves as his own pin boy.
   Caution: Children should be instructed not to step over the starting line, not to throw the ball instead of rolling it, and not to interfere with another player.

C. Teacher and Class
1. *Purpose*
   a. To improve skill of throwing and catching a ball or beanbag
   b. To learn to take turns
2. *Equipment*
   A 6-inch rubber ball or beanbag for each group of ten children
3. *Description*
   Children stand side by side, about 10 feet from the child chosen to be "teacher." The ball or beanbag is tossed by the "teacher" to the first child in line, who tosses it back to the "teacher." This procedure continues down the line. When the end of the line is reached, the first child in line becomes "teacher." The child who was "teacher" takes his place at the end of the line. The game continues until each child has been "teacher."

D. Beanbag in the Triangle

1. *Purpose*
   a. To improve skill of tossing a beanbag into a given target
   b. To learn to follow directions
2. *Equipment*
   Four beanbags
3. *Description*
   The following diagram is drawn on the floor. Six or eight children stand, one behind the other, at a distance of 8 feet from the diagram. Each child throws two beanbags, one after another, into the triangle. Players score 3 points for each beanbag that is tossed into section 3 (the smallest section of the triangle), 2 points for section 2, and 1 point for section 1. The child receiving the highest score wins.

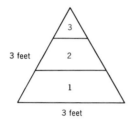

Caution: Children should be instructed not to interfere with other children and not to step over the line while tossing the beanbag.

RHYTHMIC ACTIVITIES

A program of rhythmic activities for children of elementary-school age should include a systematic progression of the materials which contribute to the development of rhythmic response and skill in rhythmic movement. The program should establish in children the ability to move easily in varied activity patterns which involve neuromuscular coordinations suitable to the age and ability of the children. Five- and six-year-olds possess tremendous physical drive. Because of this, the activities which comprise the rhythmic program should be vigorous. But because the attention span of these young children is short, each activity should be of short duration. At this age there is a great need to use the large-muscle groups; therefore rhythmic-movement patterns should be planned to meet this need.

Children gain an understanding of the importance of rhythm as they experiment with ways of moving their bodies, as they observe others move, as they watch the movement of animals and various animate objects, and as they discuss these various ways of moving. A careful teacher helps children to communicate more effectively and to enjoy adventure through movement. Higher standards of appreciation become established as children's skills develop. Only with basic understanding will real learning in rhythmic activity take place. As children learn to move with easy, flowing rhythm, tensions disappear, and improvement in posture often results. Correct body movements, learned early in life, contribute to the enrichment of living and provide basic skills for many recreational activities utilized in later years.

Children in the primary grades of elementary school enjoy experimenting with fundamental movements, such as walking, running, skipping, sliding, hopping, and galloping. They learn to combine these movements as they create their own dance patterns. Children of varied abilities enjoy participating in a widely varied selection of activities. Some like best to interpret the mood of musical selections. Others prefer to create a movement pattern and then combine it with music. Most young folk enjoy singing games. In planning and teaching rhythmic activities, it is well to remember that:

1. Children delight in activity. Too much waiting for a turn while others are active interferes with attention and creates behavior problems.

2. The music selected to accompany rhythmic activities should be simple and understandable to children. Music should be played with clear accent, but without overemphasis on the beat.

3. Periods of vigorous activity should be brief and should be followed by relaxation periods.

4. Children enjoy the opportunity to express originality and individuality.

The rhythms, singing games, and simple dances included in this chapter as suggested materials of instruction for children of the five- and six-year-old group have been selected with the above four principles in mind. Music for these activities will be found in the Appendix. A list of suggested recordings appears at the end of Part Two, pages 218 and 219.

Rhythms

1. **Fundamental Rhythms**
   a. Walking
   b. Running
   c. Skipping
   d. Hopping
   e. Galloping
   f. Sway and twist
   g. Swing
2. **Rhythm Combinations**
   a. Walk and bow
   b. Walk and hop
   c. Run and jump
3. **Time and Space Concepts**
   a. Up and down (level)
   b. Round and round (direction)
   c. Fast and slow

Figure 5–3. Up and Down (also Seesaw)

4. **Interpretive Rhythms—Animals**
   a. Ducks
   b. Camels
   c. Horses
   d. Birds
   e. Elephants
   f. Kangaroos

Figure 5–4.
Camels

Figure 5–5.
Elephants

Figure 5–6.
Kangaroos

5. **Interpretive Rhythms—Characters**
   a. Giants
   b. Dwarfs
   c. Witches
   d. Fairies
6. **Play Rhythms**
   a. Swings
   b. Seesaws
   c. Tops
   d. Bicycles
   e. Rowboats

Figure 5–7. Giants

Figure 5–8.
Dwarfs

Figure 5–9.
Swings

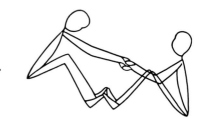

Figure 5–10. Rowboats

Singing Games and Dances

THE MUFFIN MAN

1. Do you know the muffin man, the muffin man, the
       muffin man,
   Do you know the muffin man, who lives in Drury
       Lane?
2. Yes, I know the muffin man, the muffin man, the muffin
       man,
   Yes, I know the muffin man who lives in Drury Lane.
3. Two of us know the muffin man, the muffin man, the
       muffin man,
   Two of us know the muffin man who lives in Drury
       Lane.

Step

   Skipping step

Position

   Four children are chosen to stand in the corners of the room.
   The other children stand in a single circle, all facing the center.

The Dance

   1. The children in the corners of the room skip out, and each
      one chooses a partner.
   2. The partners join hands and skip back to the corners.
   3. The partners join hands and skip around each other.

DID YOU EVER SEE A LASSIE

   Did you ever see a lassie, a lassie, a lassie
   Did you ever see a lassie do this way and that?
   Do this way and that way, do this way and that way,
   Did you ever see a lassie do this way and that?

Step

   Walking step

Position

   Single circle with hands joined. One child stands in the center
   of the circle.

The Dance

The children walk around counterclockwise, singing the first two lines of the song, while the child in the center does a simple stunt in time with the music.

As they sing the last two lines of the song, all children imitate the child in the center.

At the end of the song the child who was in the center chooses another child to go into the center of the circle. It is desirable for boys to choose girls and girls to choose boys. When a boy goes into the center, the word "laddie" should be substituted for the word "lassie."

TWO LITTLE BLACKBIRDS

Two little blackbirds sitting on a hill,
One named Jack, the other named Jill.
Fly away, Jack, fly away, Jill,
Come back, Jack, come back, Jill.

Step

Running step

Position

Double circle, partners facing

The Dance

As the children sing the first line they stoop down on the words "sitting on a hill."

In the second line, when Jack's name is mentioned, the boys jump up and stoop again.

When Jill's name is mentioned, the girls jump up and stoop again.

On the words "fly away, Jack," the boys imitate birds and fly away from the circle.

On the words "fly away, Jill," the girls fly away.

On the words "come back, Jack," the boys fly back to their places.

On the words "come back, Jill," the girls fly back.

Repeat the whole song, singing "tra, la, la," and all skip.

PUNCHINELLO

1. Look who is here, Punchinello, funny fellow.
   Look who is here, Punchinello, funny clown.
2. What can you do, Punchinello, funny fellow,
   What can you do, Punchinello, funny clown?
3. We'll do it too, Punchinello, funny fellow,
   We'll do it too, Punchinello, funny clown.
4. Whom do you choose, Punchinello, funny fellow,
   Whom do you choose, Punchinello, funny clown?

Step

Walking step

Position

Single circle with hands joined, all facing the center. One child in the center of the circle is Punchinello.

The Dance

1. Children walk around the circle counterclockwise.
2. They walk around the circle again, while Punchinello does some simple stunt or trick.
3. Everyone imitates Punchinello.
4. Punchinello closes his eyes and turns around and around while the other children sing the last verse. The child to whom Punchinello points at the end of the verse becomes the next Punchinello.

A-HUNTING WE WILL GO

Oh, a-hunting we will go, a-hunting we will go,
We'll catch a fox and put him in a box and then
we'll let him go.
Tra, la, la, la, la, la, la,
Tra, la, la, la, la, la,
Tra, la, la, la, la, la, la, la, la, la,
Tra, la, la, la, la, la.

Step

Skipping step

Position

Long sets of four couples, partners standing side by side, and all facing the head of the set

The Dance

Verse. First couple in each set cross hands, skip down the center of the set, and return. The others clap hands lightly as they sing the verse.

Chorus. All cross hands and skip, following the head couple, who turn to the left and skip to the foot of the set. When they reach this position the head couple form an arch with their arms, and all the others skip under the arch, returning to original places. The second couple is now the head couple, and the couple who started out as the head couple now stands at the foot of the set.

Repeat the whole dance until each couple has a turn at being the head couple.

THE MULBERRY BUSH

1. Here we go round the mulburry bush, the mulberry bush, the mulberry bush,
   Here we go round the mulberry bush so early in the morning.
2. This is the way we wash our clothes, wash our clothes, wash our clothes,
   This is the way we wash our clothes so early Monday morning.
3. This is the way we iron our clothes, etc.
4. This is the way we scrub the floor, etc.
5. This is the way we mend our clothes, etc.
6. This is the way we sweep the house, etc.
7. Thus we play when our work is done, etc.

Steps

Walking step, skipping step

Position

Single circle with hands joined

The Dance

As the children sing the first verse, they walk around the circle counterclockwise.

As each verse is sung, the pantomime suits the action suggested by the words.

The first verse is repeated after every other verse.

As the last verse is sung, the children skip around the circle.

I WISH I HAD A WINDMILL

1.   I wish I had a windmill, a windmill, a windmill,
      I wish I had a windmill, I know what I'd have it do.
2.   I'd have it draw the water, the water, the water,
      I'd have it draw the water up from the river below.
3.   I'd have it make a duck pond, a duck pond, a duck
         pond,
      I'd have it make a duck pond so ducks and geese could
         swim.
4.   The ducks will make their wings flap, their wings flap,
         their wings flap,
      The ducks will make their wings flap, then they will
         say, "quack, quack."
5.   The geese will stretch their necks out, their necks out,
         their necks out,
      The geese will stretch their necks out, then they will
         say, "s-s-s-s."

Steps
   Walking for verse 1, duck walk for verse 4, arms folded and stretched forward for verse 5

Position
   Single circle with hands joined for the first verse
   The circle moves counterclockwise

The Dance
   1. Walk around circle, singing.
   2. Join hands with partners or in small groups and move arms like windmills.
   3. Walk around in small groups to represent duck ponds.
   4. Walk like ducks.
   5. Fold hands and stretch arms forward like geese.

THE FARMER IN THE DELL

1.	The farmer in the dell, The farmer in the dell, Heigh-o the derry-o, The farmer in the dell.
2.	The farmer takes a wife, etc.
3.	The wife takes the child, etc.
4.	The child takes the nurse, etc.
5.	The nurse takes the dog, etc.
6.	The dog takes the cat, etc.
7.	The cat takes the rat, etc.
8.	The rat takes the cheese, etc.
9.	They're all in the dell, etc.
10.	The farmer goes away, etc.
11.	The wife goes away, etc.
12.	The child goes away, etc.
13.	The nurse goes away, etc.
14.	The dog goes away, etc.
15.	The cat goes away, etc.
16.	The rat goes away, etc.
17.	The cheese stands alone, etc.

Step

Walking step

Position

Single circle, hands joined

The Dance

As they sing the first verse, the children walk around the circle. The farmer, who stands in the center of the circle, chooses another child to be the wife.

As they sing the second verse, the wife chooses another child to be the child.

This continues through all the verses. The children continue to walk around the circle, and the selection goes on.

When the ninth verse is sung, the children all walk around the circle, with those who are in the center walking in a smaller circle of their own.

Beginning with the tenth verse, as the children walk around

the circle, the child in the center who represents the character mentioned in the verse leaves the center of the circle and returns to his own place in the large circle.

As the seventeenth verse is sung, the children stand and clap their hands in time to the music, singing, "The cheese stands alone," etc.

The child who was the cheese becomes the next farmer.

LOOBY LOO

Chorus

> Here we go Looby Loo, here we go Looby Light
> Here we go Looby Loo, all on a Saturday night.

Verse

1. I put my right hand in, I put my right hand out,
    I give my hand a shake, shake, shake, and turn myself
        about.
2. I put my left hand in, I put my left hand out,
    I give my hand a shake, shake, shake, and turn myself
        about.
3. I put my right foot in, I put my right foot out,
    I give my foot a shake, shake, shake, and turn myself
        about.
4. I put my left foot in, I put my left foot out,
    I give my foot a shake, shake, shake, and turn myself,
        about.
5. I put my whole self in, I put my whole self out,
    I give myself a shake, shake, shake, and turn myself
        about.

Steps

Walking step, skipping step

Position

Single circle, hands joined

The Dance

While singing the chorus, which precedes each verse, the children walk or skip around the circle, moving counterclockwise.

While singing the verses, the children stand in a circle and act out the suggestions of the words.

STUNTS AND SELF-TESTING ACTIVITIES

Children in the five- and six-year-old group need and are interested in physical activities which contribute to the development of strong muscles and neuromuscular coordinations. The large muscles of children in this age group are more completely developed than the smaller, or accessory muscles. In order that the program of physical education adequately serve these children, there should be provision for a variety of vigorous activities, which bring into use as many different muscle groups as possible.

Simple stunts and self-testing activities provide exercise which promotes muscle development. Stunts and self-testing activities also make it possible for children to evaluate their own learning—to recognize success, to see improvement, to acknowledge their limitations. In this chapter, stunts and self-testing activities are classified under four definite headings. The suggestions which follow clarify the classifications and list sample activities. No attempt is made to provide detailed materials for a complete program of stunts and self-testing activities; however, the teacher who wishes to round out the program should experience little difficulty if the activities suggested here are used as a guide.

1. **Development of Arm and Shoulder Muscles**
   a. Swinging on rings or high bars.
   b. Rope climbing.
   c. Throwing balls and beanbags.
   d. Climbing on climbing apparatus.
2. **Development of Leg and Back Muscles**
   a. Jumping. In place, in stride position, forward and back.
   b. Running.
   c. Bicycling. Lying on back, with knees bent up over chests, make circles with legs as though riding a bicycle.
3. **Development of Abdominal and Lateral Trunk Muscles**
   a. Logrolling. Lying on back across one end of a rug, with arms at sides, knees straight and feet together, roll slowly over and over to other end of rug without using hands; roll evenly so that body remains on the rug.
   b. Modified forward roll. Standing at one end of rug, with feet in stride position, hands on the rug between the feet,

fingertips toward each other, roll the body forward and over by touching head to hands.
   c. Leg raising. Lying on back, raise legs alternately.
4. Development of Balance for Body Control
   a. Climbing ladders or steps.
   b. Hopping. On one foot, on both feet.
   c. Tiptoe walk.

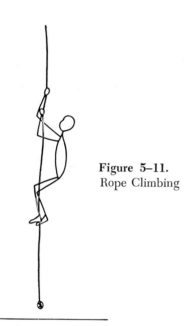

Figure 5–11.
Rope Climbing

Knot 6 inches from floor

Figure 5–12. Forward Roll

SUMMARY

This chapter explains the ways in which a physical education program may be planned to meet the needs of five- and six-year-old children. It suggests materials which may be used to advantage in such a program, but it makes no attempt to outline all the activities required to make the program complete. The success of the program may be evaluated by checking the actual outcomes against the following list of desirable outcomes:
   1. Is the child developing a wholesome attitude toward self?

2. Does this program include learnings which envelop the whole child?

3. Is the program free from monotonous routine?

4. Does the program provide for development of both large- and small-muscle groups?

5. Is there evidence of a systematic progression of skills in all areas?

If the preceding suggested outcomes have been achieved, then children are ready for the activities suggested in the next chapter.

SUGGESTED ACTIVITY UNIT

Develop an activity unit based on the dramatization of Christmas toys or a toy shop. Plan rhythmic selections to be used, possible interpretations of movements of the toys, and ways in which the activities may be supplemented and enriched by other subjects, especially language arts, music, and art.

6. Program for the
Seven- and Eight-year-olds

Knowledge of the physical and emotional characteristics of children of any age group is helpful only when it is used intelligently. It must be remembered that nature performs no magic in a child's development on the specific date when the calendar moves him on to the next age group. Rather, the changes that growth and development bring are constantly in process; in many cases they are so gradual that they sometimes are scarcely noticed.

Growth and Development Are Gradual Processes. As the teacher considers the characteristics of seven- and eight-year-old children, he must reflect on the dominant traits of the six-year-olds as well as the characteristics which will appear in the nine-year-olds. Unless he does this he will find it difficult to provide a school program that is sufficiently flexible for the wide range of needs and abilities within his own group of children. The teacher must always keep in mind that children develop according to individual patterns as well as according to the average and ex- pected growth patterns for the age group to which they belong.

Seven- and eight-year-old children strongly resemble six-year- old children in certain ways of development. They continue, as do the six-year-olds, to grow physically at a slow and steady pace. During the years between six and eight, the average yearly in- crease in height is 2 to 3 inches and the gain in weight is 3 to 6 pounds. Legs and arms lengthen, and hands grow larger. The development of large-muscle coordinations continues, but skill in the use of small muscles also becomes established. These children hold and use writing and drawing tools more comfortably and efficiently. Eye muscles develop to a degree which makes these children ready for activities involving the use of both close and

102

distant vision. Hand-eye coordinations improve at this age in most children. Temporary teeth are being replaced by permanent teeth. Six-year molars, incisors, and lower bicuspids appear.

In general, children of the seven- and eight-year-old group are active, vivacious, and energetic. They sustain energy over a longer period than do their younger brothers and sisters. Children in this age group show a definite interest in others. They begin to participate in cooperative planning and to select their friends from members of their own sex. Boys will associate naturally with boys, and girls with girls. These children enjoy group organization. They seek thrilling adventures and experiences. They strive to win—to be first. They are sensitive to the reaction of others toward them and their accomplishments. They seek adult approval and praise. They show improvement in self-control. The attention span of seven- and eight-year-old children is longer, and their interest more sustained. In these children there is great zeal and eagerness to attack new problems, greater curiosity, keener power of observation, increased skill in self-evaluation, a more fervent interest in people.

The Needs of These Children. Children seven and eight years of age require active play for the continued development of their large muscles. They need skillfully guided training for the development of small muscles. Rest and relaxation periods should be recognized as important to daily routine. A change of activity often serves as the most desirable type of relaxation for children in this age group. Even though the ability to sustain interest has increased for the majority of seven- and eight-year-olds, teachers should be ever aware of the need to provide frequent opportunities for rest and relaxation.

Seven- and eight-year-old children require a school program that challenges their mental capacities as well as fulfilling their physical and emotional needs. Just to be physically active is not enough. Activity must have real purpose and meaning—it must make children think as well as move about.

In physical education, teachers of young children have excellent resources from which to select materials for the school program. There are almost unlimited numbers of games and self-testing activities which provide opportunity to develop stronger muscles, better balance, greater agility, and satisfactory coordinations. There are games and stunts which can satisfy children's interest in competition. There are rhythms and dances which provide opportunity for vigorous physical activity and which, at the same time, stimulate children's interest in the aesthetic areas. There are physical education activities which help children to recognize their own abilities, to set standards, to play cooperatively, to compete fairly, and to improve skills. Through physical education children may receive much fundamental education which is conducive to satisfactory total adjustment to their environment. If taught well and with sound guidance techniques, many physical education activities result in pleasant and enjoyable situations and experiences for children.

A Third-grade Unit of Instruction. An enjoyable and profitable situation developed in a third-grade classroom. Two boys volunteered to demonstrate some Indian dance steps which they had learned at the Indian Folklore Club. The teacher did not make the suggestion that this demonstration take place. It was the children's idea. The boys who had attended the club meeting and learned the Indian dance steps made tom-toms to accompany their dancing. These boys shared with the other children in their class the information and knowledge they had acquired through this interesting experience at the club. Learning the Indian dance steps motivated an interest in learning some Indian songs, and learning the songs helped to arouse the children's curiosity about other phases of Indian lore. What started out to be a simple demonstration of Indian dance steps laid a foundation for a challenging and worthwhile social studies unit in which numerous physical activities were included.

When the children in this class expressed their desire to study Indian lore, the teacher began at once to make careful plans for a unit of instruction. She proposed that the center of interest be a trading post. The children were delighted with this suggestion, and the unit was introduced with a discussion of problems relating to a trading post. Groups of children were organized to seek information, to construct properties, and to select activities. These seven- and eight-year-old children soon became as enthusiastic as the five- and six-year-olds in the rodeo unit. They learned Indian dances relating to war, harvest, and peace. They acted out the smoking of the peace pipe. They competed in feats of strength and speed and played games which involved accuracy in throwing. They beat rhythms on the tom-toms which the boys had made. They participated in interpretive rhythms, such as walking quietly through the forest, stalking animals in the hunt for food, and running nimbly and quickly. Through practice they developed considerable skill in these activities.

While participating in the physical activities in this unit, the children acquired much knowledge of the customs of American Indians, of the relations between Indians and early white settlers in this country, and of trading posts which made possible an exchange of goods and information between the two groups. The trading-post activities, which served as the starting point and culmination of this study, summarized important new learnings and valuable associations of ideas. They helped to create favorable attitudes toward Indians and developed an appreciation for Indian folklore. The terms "playing Indian" and "playing store" now had greater meaning for these children. They really understood what they were doing when they play-acted daily activities which were a part of Indian life. Though physical education activities were prominent in this unit, there were also numerous language, music, and art activities which provided for natural and desirable integration of learnings.

Such units of instruction not only provide interesting opportunities for integration but also establish the motivation for practice, which is necessary for satisfactory development of a variety of skills in games, self-testing activities, stunts, rhythms, and dances. Children of this age group need much practice in games which contribute to systematic growth in the ability to follow directions, to work in prescribed formations, and to play in small groups within which children help each other. These children also need opportunities to improve their speed in running and their skill in jumping and in throwing, catching, batting, and dodging a ball. They should have, too, the fun of playing games and participating in other activities they learned when they were younger. If physical education does not provide fun, it fails in its mission.

GAMES

The games described and listed below fulfill the needs just stated. Together with rhythmic activities and self-testing activities, they comprise a sound program of physical education for children in the seven- and eight-year-old group.

Outdoor—Large-group Games

A. Single Dodge Ball
1. *Purpose*
   a. To improve skill in throwing and catching a ball
   b. To learn to dodge
2. *Equipment*
   A 6-inch rubber ball
3. *Description*
   Children form a single circle, facing the center. Three or four children stand in the center of the circle. The children in the circle throw the ball, trying to strike the children who are in the center. These children dodge to avoid being struck. When a child is struck, he changes places with the child who struck him.
   Caution: The ball should be thrown to hit below the waist.

B. Stride Ball
1. *Purpose*
   To teach children to be alert and to move quickly
2. *Equipment*
   A 6-inch rubber ball
3. *Description*
   Players form a single circle, stride position, the feet of each player touching the feet of his neighbor. The child who is "it" stands in the center of the circle. One of the players has the ball. The players roll the ball from one to the other. "It" tries to seize the ball and roll it out of the circle between the feet of one of the players. Players may use their hands to guard the openings but may not move their feet. When the ball passes between the feet of a player, that player becomes "it." If the ball goes out of

the circle between two players, the one on whose right it goes out becomes "it."

Figure 6–1. Stride Ball

C. Red Light

1. *Purpose*

    a. To develop self-control

    b. To learn to move quickly

2. *Equipment*

    None

3. *Description*

    Children stand side by side in a starting line facing "it." "It" stands on a goal line 30 feet away from the starting line, with his back turned to the other players. "It" counts to ten, then shouts, "Red light," and quickly turns around to face the other players. The other players start to run toward the goal line, but must stand still when "it" turns around. If "it" sees any player move, that player must go back to the starting line and begin again. The game continues until one player reaches the goal line. This player then becomes "it."

D. Sky Ball

1. *Purpose*
   a. To increase skill in throwing a ball
   b. To increase skill in catching a ball
2. *Equipment*
   A 6-inch rubber ball
3. *Description*
   Two teams of even size scatter over the playing space. No player may stand in the neutral area.

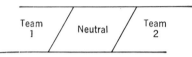

A player from one team throws the ball over the neutral area. A team scores 1 point for each ball caught. The player who catches or picks up the ball throws it back to his opponents. A team loses a point if a player throws the ball into the neutral area.

E. Bases on Balls

1. *Purpose*
   a. To learn to kick a ball
   b. To increase speed in running
2. *Equipment*
   A soccer ball or a 6-inch rubber ball, a baseball diamond with base lines of 25 feet
3. *Description*
   The group is divided into two teams of even size. The players on each team line up side by side, one team on either side of home plate. The players on each team are numbered in order. Number 1 player on one team, now called the kicking team, stands behind home plate. Number 1 player on the other team, now called the fielding team, takes his place anywhere in the field. The kicker places the ball on home plate, takes one step, and kicks the ball. If the ball is fair, landing between first and third bases, the kicker runs to first base and continues around the other bases until the fielder recovers the ball, runs to home plate,

and places the ball there. The kicker receives 1 point for each base he touches before the fielder places the ball on home plate. The kicker may have two trials to kick a fair ball.

Players on the kicking team kick in order and players on the fielding team field in order until five players have had turns at kicking; then teams change positions. This play continues until all players have had turns at kicking and fielding. The team with the higher score wins. A kicker who kicks two foul balls is out.

F. **Bat Ball**
  1. *Purpose*
    a. To improve skill in running
    b. To improve skill in dodging
    c. To learn to hit a moving target
    d. To learn to bat a ball
    e. To improve skill in catching
  2. *Equipment*
    A volleyball or 10-inch rubber ball, a field about 40 by 60 feet, a base
  3. *Description*
    The class is divided into two teams of even size. One team assigns its players to positions in the field, and the other team lines up behind the service line. The players are numbered in order.

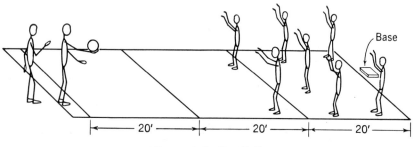

20'   20'   20'

Figure 6–2. Bat Ball

The server stands with both feet behind the service line. He holds the ball in one hand and bats it with the other.

He may bat with a closed or open hand. He also may toss the ball and bat it with both hands, either open or closed. He must bat the ball across the first 20-foot line. He is entitled to two tries, but if he fails on the second, he is out. A run is scored each time a batter makes a good serve and succeeds in running around the base to home plate without being tagged by the ball. A batter is out if his serve is caught. Fielders may leave the playing area to retrieve a ball, but must return to the boundary line before throwing it. One point is scored for each run. Only the batting team scores. When three outs are made the teams exchange positions.

Outs: An out is made when (*a*) the ball on the fly is caught by a fielder; (*b*) the batter fails to serve the ball into the field; (*c*) the ball is thrown to the base ahead of the runner; (*d*) the batter fails to run around the base and home without being tagged; (*e*) the runner steps over the boundary line; (*f*) the runner is tagged by a ball thrown by a fielder.

Fouls: A foul is made when (*a*) a member of the fielding team takes more than one step while holding the ball; (*b*) a fielder bounces the ball and catches it himself; (*c*) a fielder holds the ball more than five seconds; (*d*) a fielder tags the runner with the ball before the runner crosses the first line.

G. Catch Ball

1. *Purpose*
   a. To improve skill in catching
   b. To improve skill in throwing
2. *Equipment*
   A volleyball, a space 20 by 20 feet divided into three equal parts
3. *Description*
   The class is divided into two teams of even size. The teams are arranged so that one covers each of the two outside playing spaces, leaving a neutral space in the center. The teacher calls, "Play," and throws the ball to a member of either team, who throws it over the neutral space into

the opposing team's space. The player who catches or retrieves the ball throws it over the neutral area to the other team. One point is scored by the throwing team when the ball hits the ground in the opposing team's space before it is caught. One point is scored by the receiving team when the thrower throws the ball out of bounds before it has been touched by a member of the receiving team. One point is scored by the opposing team when any player catches the ball and drops it. Every two minutes the teams should rearrange their players so that the back-line players come into the front line, and vice versa. The game is played for a period of time agreed upon by all players before the start of the play.

H. Circle Soccer
   1. *Purpose*
      a. To improve skill in kicking
      b. To develop accuracy in aiming
      c.. To learn to stop kicks made by opponents
   2. *Equipment*
      A soccer ball; two circles drawn one inside the other, outer one 25 feet in diameter, inner one 20 feet
   3. *Description* (see Figure 6–3)
      The class is divided into two teams of even size. The teams line up between the two circles, one team on either side of the diameter line. The teacher puts the ball in play by rolling it into the circle along the diameter line. The players

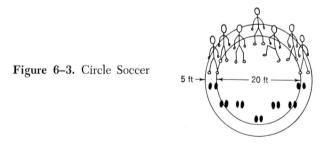

Figure 6–3. Circle Soccer

5 ft → · · ← | 20 ft →

on one team try to kick the ball past their opponents. The opponents attempt to keep the ball from passing them by blocking it with their bodies, not with their hands. One point is scored whenever the ball is kicked across the opponents' outer-circle line below the shoulders of the shortest player on the team. The team scoring the most points at the end of play wins the game.

I. Circle Chase
1. *Purpose*
   a. To learn to be alert
   b. To improve skill in running
2. *Equipment*
   None
3. *Description*
   All players but one stand side by side around a 25-foot circle. One player stands in the center of the circle. Players count off around the circle by fours, and each player keeps his number through the entire game. The player in the center of the circle calls out a number from one to four, and all players with that number run around the outside of the circle to the right, each one trying to tag the runner just ahead of him. If a player is tagged, he steps out of the circle, and the others continue to their own places. The play continues until there is one of each number left in the game. These players are the winners.

J. Follow-the-leader
1. *Purpose*
   a. To learn to be alert
   b. To learn to make quick changes of direction, position, gait, speed, etc.
2. *Equipment*
   None
3. *Description*
   The class is divided into groups of eight to ten. Each group lines up behind a leader. The boundaries of the playing space should be agreed upon before the game starts. All players must remain within the boundaries. Each leader starts to travel through the playing space by walking, running, or moving in any way he chooses. The players in each line imitate their leader. They must change their way of

moving immediately when he does. Any player who fails to do this leaves the game. After three children have been eliminated, the leader selects a new leader from the children still in the game, and the children who had been eliminated return to the game.

K. **Uncle Sam**
1. *Purpose*
   a. To learn to be alert
   b. To learn to recognize colors quickly
   c. To learn to follow directions
2. *Equipment*
   None
3. *Description*
   Children line up in a row, facing a child who is "it." "It" stands in front of a line 20 feet away, facing the group. In unison, the children chant:

> Uncle Sam, Uncle Sam,
> May we cross
> Your river dam?

"It" replies:

> Yes, you may,
> Yes, you may,
> If you have
> The color I say.

He names a color, and the children scan their clothing quickly. If the color named appears anywhere in their apparel, they may walk across the line. If they do not have the color called, they must run across, trying to avoid being caught. The child caught then becomes "it."

L. **Group Tag**
1. *Purpose*
   a. To develop speed in running
   b. To develop skill in dodging
2. *Equipment*
   None
3. *Description*
   The class is divided into groups of not more than five players. Two players do not join groups; one of these is the

runner, the other the chaser. When the game starts, the players in each group stand one behind the other in lines. The runner avoids being tagged by attaching himself to the end of any of the lines. When a player joins a group, the first player in the group must become the runner. If the chaser tags the runner before the runner attaches himself to a group, he becomes the chaser, and the chaser becomes the runner.

Outdoor—Small-group Games

A. Numbers Change
1. *Purpose*
   To develop quick response to a signal
2. *Equipment*
   None
3. *Description*
   The class is divided into groups of not more than twelve players. Each group forms a single circle, with all players facing center. The players in each circle are numbered in order. One player goes into the center of each circle and becomes the leader. Each leader calls two numbers. The players whose numbers were called exchange places. While they are doing this the leader tries to take one of their places. The player whose place is taken becomes the next leader. For variation, the players' names may be used instead of numbers.

B. Circle Hopscotch
1. *Purpose*
   a. To improve skill in throwing at a target
   b. To learn to hop without touching the lines of a diagram
   c. To learn to follow the rules of the game
2. *Equipment*
   A small stone or a puck
3. *Description* (see Figure 6–4)
   The diagram is drawn on the ground. Each player in turn:
   a. Tosses the stone into space 1, hops into the space on one foot, and kicks the stone out.
   b. Tosses the stone into space 2, hops into the space and

kicks the stone out, hops back into space 1, then out.

c. Tosses the stone into space 3, hops in on one foot and kicks the stone out, jumps to stride position in spaces 1 and 2, then out.

d. Tosses stone into space 4, hops in and kicks stone out, jumps to stride position in spaces 2 and 3, hops on one foot into space 1, then out.

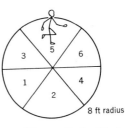

Figure 6–4. Circle Hopscotch

e. Tosses stone into space 5, jumps to stride position in spaces 1 and 2, then in 3 and 4, hops on one foot into space 5, kicks the stone out, and returns.

f. Tosses stone into space 6, jumps to stride position in spaces 1 and 2, then in 3 and 4, hops on one foot into space 5, then into space 6, kicks the stone out, and returns.

g. Jumps to stride position in spaces 1 and 2, then in 3 and 4, then 5 and 6, turns about, and returns.

Fouls: It is a foul to (*a*) step on a line; (*b*) let the stone rest on a line; (*c*) touch the ground with any part of the body other than the foot on which the player is hopping.

C. Ladder Ball

1. *Purpose*

To learn to roll a ball accurately and move quickly

2. *Equipment*

A 6-inch rubber ball

3. *Description* (see Figure 6–5)

The diagram is drawn on the ground; the starting line is 3 feet from the diagram. Each player in turn does the following:

Figure 6–5.
Ladder Ball

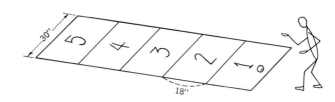

   a. Rolls the ball into space 1
   b. Runs into space 1 and retrieves the ball before it rolls out
   c. Returns to starting position
   d. Repeats this in each space

   Scoring: Each player scores one point every time he successfully retrieves the ball from a space.

D. Ladder Hopscotch

   1. *Purpose*
      a. To improve skill in throwing a puck accurately
      b. To learn to hop on one foot without stepping on a line
   2. *Equipment*
      A small stone, a small piece of wood, or a rubber heel to use as a puck
   3. *Description* (see Figure 6–5)
      The starting line is 3 feet from the diagram. Each player in turn throws the puck into space 1, hops after it on one foot, picks it up, and hops back to the starting line. The same procedure is followed in each of the spaces. The player who successfully completes the routine in all five spaces wins. A player who commits a foul, must start over.

      Fouls: It is a foul to (*a*) step on a line; (*b*) step on the ground with the free foot.

E. Hopscotch

   1. *Purpose*
      a. To learn to take turns
      b. To learn to follow rules
      c. To develop skill of tossing a stone into a given space
      d. To develop skill in hopping without stepping on lines
   2. *Equipment*
      A small stone or a flat piece of wood
   3. *Description* (see Figure 6–6)
      The diagram is drawn or painted on the floor. Each player, in turn, takes the stone and follows the routine listed here:
      a. Throw the stone into space 1, hop into space 1, pick up the stone, and hop back to the starting line.
      b. Throw the stone into space 2, then 3, etc., through the whole diagram.

   c. In spaces 2 and 3, 5 and 6, and 8 and 9, the player jumps astride.

   d. In space 10, the player turns and hops back through the diagram just as he did in going the other way.

Fouls: It is a foul to (*a*) step on a line; (*b*) touch both feet in a one-foot area.

Penalty: (*a*) Retires that player; (*b*) on the next turn, the penalized player resumes play at the numbered area.

Figure 6–6.
Hopscotch

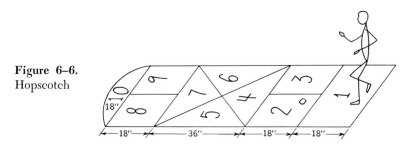

F. Pavement Ball

   1. *Purpose*

      a. To learn to roll a ball accurately into a definite area

      b. To learn to time the rolling of a ball in order to retrieve it from a definite area

   2. *Equipment*

      A 4-inch rubber ball

   3. *Description* (see Figure 6–7)

      The diagram is drawn on the ground. Each child in turn:

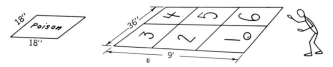

Figure 6–7. Pavement Ball

      a. Rolls the ball from the starting line into space 1, catches it before it leaves the space, and bounces it once in each space.

      b. Rolls the ball into space 2, bounces it two times in spaces 2, 3, 4, 5, 6.

c. Continues rolling and bouncing the ball in each space through 6.

d. When the ball is rolled into space 6, the player bounces it six times to finish the game, then runs to the space labeled "poison" and bounces the ball once, saying, "One game."

Fouls: It is a foul to (*a*) roll the ball into the wrong space; (*b*) fail to catch the ball before it rolls out of the space.

Penalty: Player starts over on the next turn.

Indoor—Large-group Games

A. I Say Stoop
1. *Purpose*
   a. To learn to follow directions
   b. To learn to respond quickly
2. *Equipment*
   None
3. *Description*
   Children stand in a large group. At the direction "I say stoop," all children stoop. At the direction "I say stand," all children stand.

   Fouls: It is a foul to (*a*) fail to stoop when the direction "I say stoop" is given; (*b*) fail to stand when the direction "I say stand" is given; (*c*) move when either direction is given without the words "I say" preceding it; (*d*) move before a direction is given.

   Penalty: Elimination from the game. The player who remains longest in the game wins.

B. Changing Seats
A game especially suited for use in a classroom where the furniture is permanently fixed.
1. *Purpose*
   a. To learn to follow directions quickly
   b. To learn "right" and "left"
2. *Equipment*
   None
3. *Description*
   Children sit on their chairs. The leader gives the directions

"change to the right," "change to the left," "change forward," "change backward." Children follow the directions as quickly and as accurately as possible.

C. **Days of the Week**
   1. *Purpose*
      a. To learn to wait for a signal and then follow it
      b. To learn to follow directions
      c. To improve skills in throwing and catching
   2. *Equipment*
      A 6-inch rubber ball or a beanbag
   3. *Description*
      Children sit or stand in rows, with no more than eight in a row. All face forward. Each row is given the name of a day of the week. The leader calls out the name of a day of the week and immediately throws the ball to the first child in the row with that name. The child catches the ball, throws it back to the leader, and runs around his row to the right; he then takes his position as the last one in the row. The other players in the row move forward one place. The leader continues to call the names of the various days of the week until all children have had at least one turn.

D. **Hot Ball**
   1. *Purpose*
      a. To learn to listen for a signal
      b. To learn to respond quickly
   2. *Equipment*
      A 6-inch rubber ball
   3. *Description*
      Children sit or stand in a single circle, all facing the center. The ball is passed from one child to another, either in order around the circle or from one to another in any order. This ball passing continues until the leader signals, "Stop." When this signal occurs, the child who is holding the ball receives a point. The child with the fewest points wins the game.

E. **Relay Races**
   1. *Purpose*
      a. To develop team spirit

b. To learn to wait for a signal

c. To learn to respond quickly

2. *Equipment*

None

3. *Description*

The group is divided into teams of no more than six or eight children. When the starting signal is heard, the first child in each team runs to a location equally distant for all teams, returns to place, and tags the next child, who then becomes the runner. Base should be placed away from walls or furniture for safety.

The first team to have all members correctly complete the activity and return to the agreed finish position wins.

Simple relay-race formation: Objects to run around.

```
              Starting Line
0        X  X  X  X  X  X      T
0        X  X  X  X  X  X      E
0        X  X  X  X  X  X      A
0        X  X  X  X  X  X      M
0        X  X  X  X  X  X      S
```

Each runner, in turn, runs around an object, such as a chair, a block of wood, or a person, returns to his place, tags the next runner, and then goes to the end of the line.

Shuttle relay:

```
10  8  6  4  2        1  3  5  7  9
X   X  X  X  X        X  X  X  X  X
X   X  X  X  X        X  X  X  X  X
X   X  X  X  X        X  X  X  X  X
```

The first runner in each team (number 1) starts the race. He runs to the line opposite his position and tags runner number 2, who in turn tags number 3, and so on until all runners have had a turn. When the race is finished, all runners will be behind the line directly opposite the one behind which they stood when the game started.

Many variations of the relay race may be taught. Races which involve the passing of beanbags or balls and those which provide opportunity for practice in throwing and catching are especially valuable to children in this age group.

F. Weather Cock

1. *Purpose*
   a. To learn direction
   b. To learn to follow instructions quickly and accurately

2. *Equipment*
   None

3. *Description*
   Before they play this game, children should be taught the relative locations and directions of north, south, east, and west. To play the game, children stand in an informal group. The leader calls out, "North," "South," "East," or "West." The children respond to the directions of the leader by facing north when that direction is given, south when that direction is given, etc. The leader sometimes surprises the children by calling out, "Whirlwind!" Then the children twirl around three times. The children who fail to follow directions are eliminated from the game.

   Each child who fails to follow directions receives a point, and the child who receives the fewest points wins.

Indoor—Small-group Games

A. Eraser in the Ring

1. *Purpose*
   a. To learn to throw a beanbag accurately at a target
   b. To learn to take turns
   c. To learn to play fair
   d. To learn simple scorekeeping

2. *Equipment*
   Three beanbags and a blackboard eraser

3. *Description*
   Children stand about 8 feet from the circle, in the center of which is an eraser. The children take turns throwing a beanbag underhand to knock the eraser out of the circle. Each child has three turns if he needs them. One point is scored each time the eraser goes out of the circle. The penalty for a foul is loss of turn.

Fouls: It is a foul to (*a*) step over the starting line; (*b*) interfere with another player.

B. Knockout

1. *Purpose*
   a. To learn to take turns
   b. To learn to strike an object with a bouncing ball

2. *Equipment*
   A blackboard eraser, a 6-inch rubber ball

3. *Description*
   A 3-foot square is drawn on the floor. The eraser is in the center of the square. One child stands on each side of the square. One child bounces the ball on the eraser, attempting to knock it out of the square. The eraser, if it has not been knocked out of the square, is left where it is, and each child, in turn, bounces the ball on the eraser until one is successful in knocking it out. The child who does this wins.

C. One, Two, Three, Alairy

1. *Purpose*
   a. To improve skill in bouncing and catching a ball
   b. To learn to take turns

2. *Equipment*
   Several 6-inch rubber balls

3. *Description*
   The class is divided into small groups, and each group is given a ball. The children in each group take turns bouncing the ball in time to the rhythm of the verses. Each child bounces the ball three times, the third bounce being a hard one to allow various stunts to be done. The verse is recited as follows:

   > One, two, three, alairy,
   > Four, five, six, alairy,
   > Seven, eight, nine, alairy,
   > Ten, alairy, postman.

   Figure 1. Each time the word "alairy" is spoken, the child who is bouncing the ball swings his left or right leg over the ball. As the word "postman" is spoken the child catches and holds the ball.

Figure 2. Same as Figure 1, but the other leg is swung over the ball.

Figure 3. When the word "alairy" is spoken, the ball is passed through a circle made by the child's arms and hands.

Figure 4. Same as Figure 1, but the player turns completely around before catching the ball at the end of the rhyme.

Figure 5. Same as Figure 4, but the player turns in the opposite direction.

Fouls: It is a foul to (*a*) fail to hold the ball; (*b*) fail to complete any of the routines.

Penalty: Loss of turn. On the next turn, the player starts with the stunt missed.

D. Fair and Foul

1. *Purpose*
   a. To learn to take turns
   b. To improve skill in rolling a ball between two lines
2. *Equipment*
   A 6-inch rubber ball
3. *Description*
   Two lines are drawn on the floor, 3 feet apart. Each player, in turn, stands 15 feet away and bowls the ball between the lines. A point is scored each time the ball passes between the lines without touching either line. If the ball touches a boundary line or rolls out from between the lines, the player who rolled the ball loses the ball to the next player.

E. Beanbag in the Circle

1. *Purpose*
   a. To learn to keep score
   b. To improve skill in tossing a beanbag at a target
2. *Equipment*
   Three beanbags
3. *Description*
   Two concentric circles, of 2 feet and 3 feet in diameter, are drawn on the floor. The players

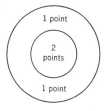

stand one behind the other, about 10 feet from the diagram. Each player, in turn, tosses three beanbags, one after the other, into the circle. There is a score of 10 points for each beanbag that lands in the inner circle and of 5 points for each one that lands in the outer circle.

F. Schoolroom Bowling

   1. *Purpose*
     a. To improve skill of rolling a ball at a target
     b. To learn to keep score
     c. To learn to take turns
   2. *Equipment*
     Bowling pins and balls. Blackboard erasers serve well if regular pins are not available; 6-inch rubber balls are satisfactory.
   3. *Description*
     Erasers are set up in three rows, as in the diagram. Each player, in turn, stands about 15 feet from the pins and rolls two balls, one after the other, in an attempt to knock down the pins. One point is scored for each pin knocked down.

     It saves time if each child takes his place in the pinsetting line after his turn at bowling.

RHYTHMS AND DANCE

Most seven- and eight-year-old children have acquired satisfactory body coordination. Their general body movements are fairly easy, purposeful, and rhythmic. As five- and six-year-olds, they enjoyed freedom of expression to musical accompaniment. Fundamental patterns of movement, such as walking, running, jumping, twisting, and turning, represented natural expression for these children. This expression fulfilled the need for activity and body expression. These natural patterns of locomotion and axial movement, which these children delighted in doing, are the basis for many dance steps and patterns. They form the background for the simple dances which seven- and eight-year-old children enjoy learning. Children who have opportunities for this type of body expression become poised and graceful. They experience satisfaction and enjoyment in rhythmic activities. Such a program stimulates physical growth and contributes to the development of standards of behavior which can be applied in social situations.

Teaching Rhythms. Teaching fundamental rhythms to seven- and eight-year-olds follows in general the plan carried on with the five- and six-year-olds. The first consideration is, naturally, the needs of the group. The methods to be used and the type of accompaniment to be selected are also important.

Before children can be expected to express mood, emotion, or feeling through the medium of body movement in response to rhythm, they must hear and feel the pulse of the music. In order to translate what they hear and feel, children must be able to distinguish the underlying beat and recognize musical phrases. Because some children do not always hear what the music says, the teacher must plan activities which provide opportunities for developing this skill.

The seven- and eight-year-olds usually recognize the musical patterns for fundamental rhythms. However, this does not mean that these children will not profit by extended experiences. Variations in interpretations stimulate interest. For example, changing the foot pattern or arm pattern varies walking and makes the activity more fun. The normal foot pattern is indicated with the walk rhythm as R L R L, R L R L, with one step for each of the underlying beats. Another walk might be a very fast walk, shown as R L R L R L R L, R L R L R L R L. Still another walk might be very slow, shown as R L R L, with one step on every second underlying beat. In addition to walking at different tempos, other walking variations add to the children's pleasure. Walking on the toes, walking with the body hunched down, walking with a heavy step or with a very light step, changing the direction of the walk as the phrases in the music change, and combining movements with holds or stops—all such variations add to the excitement and fun that experimenting with movements provides.

The arm movements for walking rhythms are a normal R L R L swing of the arms in opposition to the foot movement, as indicated under the walk music (see page 280). The arm, as well as the foot movements, may be varied. Both arms may be held above the head as the individual walks forward on the first phrase of the music, both arms lowered on the second phrase, raised again on the third, and lowered on the fourth. This pattern might be indicated as:

Feet	R L R L, R L R L	R L R L, R L R L
Arms	Up R and L	Down R and L

As children experiment with motions, many different reactions result. Observation and discussion along with their experiences help them discover acceptable ways of communicating their thoughts. The individual who discovers different possibilities in movement has learned how to use another valuable tool of expression and communication. The material included in this chapter represents the kinds of rhythmic activities and dance patterns these children should experience.

When the children have learned to listen for and to recognize the underlying beat and the parts of the musical selection, they should then listen for the phrases within the parts. Hand raising at the beginning of a phrase, moving the arms in large circles in front of the body throughout the phrase, or some other simple type of participation helps the teacher discover the ability of each child to hear intelligently. This preliminary method of listening and recognizing rhythmic patterns acquaints children with the language of music and makes locomotive movement much easier.

Informality usually provides a better learning situation when children experiment with fundamental rhythms. However, large groups of children make it necessary to teach and practice certain procedures of safety and courtesy. Necessary for a good teaching-learning climate are such habits as listening without talking, moving quietly, using the edge of the room as one-way traffic, and not touching another child when passing. Specific suggestions for teaching follow:

1. To manage a large group in a small area, divide the group and allow one section to hum with the music and tap out the

underlying beat on the floor or desk with the hands as the other group practices moving about the room. Children enjoy such an activity and willingly help devise ways to make it possible for all to participate.

2. While children rest, discuss with them the ways different children move, what they like about the movement, and what they think contributed to good movement. The children thus begin to learn careful observation. Desirable attitudes develop through such friendly discussions, and appreciations increase.

3. As the children move about the room, place those who have difficulty with such a step as the skip in the center with a good skipper on either side.

The elements of time developed by fundamental rhythm patterns form the background for more complex time concepts which will confront children as seven- and eight-year-olds. Patterns such as long step–short step and fast walk–slow walk follow the basic elementary skills. In addition to concepts of time, these children must also develop concepts of space. They must develop the ability to move their bodies in directions—up and down, round and round, forward and back.

Gaining skill in responding to fundamental musical patterns encourages children to create and interpret patterns of their own. They enjoy being fairies, giants, soldiers, and animals. Singing games and simple dances are introduced into this background with little difficulty. Experimenting with sound along with movement makes dancing more interesting to boys and girls. When children develop their own accompaniment by using a drum or tom-tom, wooden blocks, or other instruments, either alone or in combination, they have a greater interest in the activity. Piano accompaniment or phonograph records that give a definite underlying beat ensure greater success and enjoyment in rhythmic experiences.

The following pages give teaching points and directions for developing rhythmic response and describe singing games and simple dances that may be taught to seven- and eight-year-old children.

Music for all these activities is given in the Appendix. Recordings are listed at the end of Part Two, pages 218 and 219.

Rhythms

1. **Fundamental Rhythm—Walking**
   a. Walk tall.
   b. Place, do not "stamp" heel down with each new step.
   c. Walk smoothly.
   d. Watch where you are going—head up.
   e. Let arms swing easily in opposition to the feet.
   f. Carry weight forward over the outer borders of the feet.
   g. Push off with all five toes.
   h. Point toes straight ahead.
   i. Listen to the accompaniment and try to keep with it.
2. **Rhythm Combinations**
   a. Up and down
   b. Round and round
   c. Walk, walk, hop, hop, stop
   d. Run, hop, stop
   e. Long steps—short steps
   f. Swinging
   g. Sustained movement
   h. Running in phrases

Singing Games and Dances

THE THREAD FOLLOWS THE NEEDLE

The thread follows the needle,
The thread follows the needle,
In and out the needle goes,
As mother mends the children's clothes.

Parts of the Music
  Two phrases
Rhythmic Pattern
  6/8 time, counted two beats to each measure
Step
  Walking step
Position
  Ten children stand side by side in a line. The child at one end is the needle, and the one at the other end of the line is the knot. Throughout the game the children keep their hands joined.

The Dance

The needle leads, drawing the other children after him, and passes under the arms of the knot and number 9. He then continues back to his place. This makes 9 and the knot face in the opposite direction with their arms crossed in front of their bodies.

Next the needle goes under the arms of 8 and 9 and back to place.

The needle continues until all the children are facing in the opposite direction with arms crossed in front.

At a signal from the needle, the children raise their arms and turn to ravel the thread.

Figure 6–8. The Thread Follows the Needle

HOW D'YE DO, MY PARTNER

How dy'e do, my partner?
How d'ye do today?
Will you dance in the circle?
I will show you the way.

Tra, la, la, la, la, la,
Tra, la, la, la, la.
Tra, la, la, la, la, la,
Tra, la, la, la, la, la.

Parts of the Music
   One part, two phrases
Rhythmic Pattern
   3/4 time
Steps
   Bow and curtsy, skipping step

Position

Double circle, partners facing, boys on inside of circle and girls on outside.

The Dance

"How d'ye do, my partner?" Girl curtsies to boy.

"How d'ye do today?" Boy bows to girl.

"Will you dance in the circle?" Partners grasp right hands, bending to left, and look at each other through the arch.

"I will show you the way." Partners grasp left hands and look at each other through the arch.

As the children sing the chorus, they skip around the circle with inside hands joined.

RIG-A-JIG-JIG

As I was walking down the street,
Heigh-o, heigh-o, heigh-o, heigh-o,
A pretty girl I chanced to meet,
Heigh-o, heigh-o, heigh-o.

Rig-a-jig-jig and away we go,
Away we go, away we go,
Rig-a-jig-jig and away we go,
Heigh-o, heigh-o, heigh-o.

Parts of the Music

Verse, two phrases; chorus, two phrases

Rhythmic Pattern

6/8 time, counted two beats to each measure

Steps

Walking step, skipping step

Position

Children stand in a single circle facing clockwise. One child is in the center facing counterclockwise.

The Dance

Verse. All children walk around the circle. When they sing, "A pretty girl I chanced to meet," the child in the center selects one of the circle players, who joins him in the center.

Chorus. All skip around the circle.

When the verse is repeated, each of the two children in the

center chooses a new partner. The game continues until all have partners in the center circle.

Jolly is the miller boy who lives by the mill,
The wheel goes 'round with a right good will,
One hand in the hopper and the other in the sack,
The right steps forward and the left steps back.

Parts of the Music
Four phrases
Rhythmic Pattern
2/4 time, counted four beats to each measure
Step
Walking step
Position
Double circle facing counterclockwise, with extra dancer in the center
The Dance
Couples walk around the circle until they come to the words, "the right steps forward and the left steps back." Then the extra dancer steps into the circle at any point he chooses and takes a partner, while the extra person goes to the center for the next dance. Dancers on the circle follow the directions of the song, with the girls stepping forward and the boys stepping back for a new partner.

PUSH THE BUSINESS ON

We'll hire a horse and hire a gig
So all the world may have a jig,
And I'll do all that ever I can
To push the business on.

To push the business on,
To push the business on,
And I'll do all that ever I can
To push the business on.

Rhythmic Pattern
6/8 time, counted two beats to a measure

Step

Walking step

Position

Partners, with hands joined, form double circle facing counter-clockwise.

The Dance

Verse. Children walk around the circle.

Chorus. Children stand and clap hands six times during first phrase. On second phrase, partners join both hands and walk around each other to the right. Girls move ahead to the next partner.

SEVEN STEPS (or Seven Jumps)

This dance may be too difficult for some children of this age group.

Parts of the Music

A, two phrases; B, two phrases; C, chords only

Rhythmic Pattern

4/4 time, with four beats to the measure, one to each quarter note

Steps

Step-hop (a step, then a hop on the same foot)

A jump and a turn in the opposite direction

Series of stunts

Position

Single circle, with hands joined, facing center

The Dance

1. On phrase 1 of part A of the music, four step-hops to the left, starting with the left foot.

   On phrase 2, three step-hops, continuing in the same direction, then a jump on both feet, reversing direction.

2. On phrase 1 of part B, four step-hops in the circle to the right, starting back with the right foot.

   On phrase 2, three step-hops, continuing in the same direction; then, with a high jump on the last note, face the center.

3. On chord 1 of part C, place hands on hips and raise the right foot by bending the knee at a right angle.

   On chord 2, lower the foot to the floor. Be ready to repeat 1 and 2 of the dance.

The dance repeats seven times. Each time the dance repeats, one more stunt is added. The musician varies the time of the chords so that the dancers must stay alert. Each time the dance repeats, two more chords are added.

The additional stunts: (2) raise left knee; (3) kneel on right knee; (4) kneel on left knee; (5) place right elbow on floor with chin resting in hand; (6) place left elbow on floor, with chin resting on both hands; (7) touch head to floor.

BOW, BOW, BELINDA

Verse 1	*Directions*
Step and step and bow, Belinda	Walk two steps toward partner and bow.
Step and step and bow, Belinda	Walk two steps away from partner and bow.
Step and step and bow, Belinda	Walk two steps toward partner and bow.
Won't you be my partner?	Walk two steps away from partner and bow.

Verse 2	
Right hands round and swing, Belinda	Step forward, with right hands joined, and skip around partner three times.
Right hands round and swing, Belinda	
Right hands round and swing, Belinda	
Won't you be my partner?	Return to place and bow.

Verse 3	
Left hands round and swing, Belinda	Step forward with left hands joined and skip around partner three times.
Left hands round and swing, Belinda	
Left hands round and swing, Belinda	
Won't you be my partner?	Return to place and bow.

Verse 4

Two hands round and swing, Belinda Step forward, with both hands joined, and skip around partner three times.

Two hands round and swing, Belinda

Two hands round and swing, Belinda

Won't you be my partner?   Return to place and bow.

Verse 5

Back to back and back, Belinda   Step forward and move around partner back to back three times.

Back to back and back, Belinda

Back to back and back, Belinda

Won't you be my partner?   Return to place and bow.

Verse 6

Skip and skip and skip, Belinda   With inside hands joined, skip around partner.

Skip and skip and skip, Belinda

Skip and skip and skip, Belinda

Won't you be my partner?   Return to place and bow.

CHIMES OF DUNKIRK

Rhythmic Pattern
   2/4 time
Position
   Partners facing in double circle
The Dance
   1. Three stamps—right, left, right; clap hands three times; partners join both hands and turn in place with seven running steps (measures 1 to 8 played through twice).
      Repeat all.
   2. Partners standing side by side, with inside hands joined, skip around the circle, two steps to a measure (measures 9 to 16).
   3. Same as 1, but not repeated.

STUNTS AND SELF-TESTING ACTIVITIES

Through participation in suitable stunts and self-testing activities, seven- and eight-year-olds develop better body balance and flexibility in movement and greater self-confidence. The nature of these activities promotes interest in individual progress. The competition that exists shows the child how his power and ability of today compare with his strength and agility of yesterday. The child recognizes his progress through planned activities in developing natural physical skills. He recognizes the advantages gained by practicing and developing these skills and he measures his success by the improved ways he now uses these body skills. The stunts and activities described for the development of balance and for the development of arm and shoulder muscles and body and trunk muscles fulfill the child's desire for activity and satisfactory body movement. Because this type of physical activity is objective, children themselves can check and evaluate their progress in terms of individual growth.

In planning this section of the physical education program for the seven- and eight-year-olds, the teacher should review and re-teach, if necessary, the activities developed in the previous grades. Unless the child's muscular development and coordination enable him to perform the basic stunts satisfactorily, he is not ready for activities which demand stronger and more refined muscle development. The material presented should challenge these children. It should stimulate them to greater effort.

1. **Exercises for Development of Arm and Shoulder Muscles**
    a. Review of swinging and traveling on horizontal bars and ladders.
    b. Seal walk. Children walk on their hands, hands placed on floor shoulder width apart, body and legs extended back, and legs dragging.
    c. Chinning. Children chin themselves on chinning bar.
    d. Wring the dishrag. Two children join both hands and turn under arms.

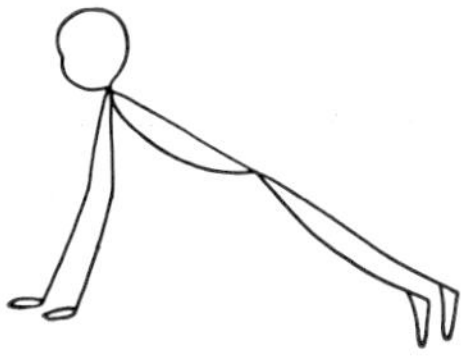

Figure 6–9.
Seal Walk

Figure 6–10.
Wring the Dishrag

2. **Exercises for Development of Legs and Back**
   a. Stiff-legged walk. Walk without bending the knees.
   b. Jump. Stand facing one side of room, with arms raised to left. Jump sideward to right and swing arms to right. Repeat to left, then forward, then backward.
   c. Backward kick. Hop in place on both feet five times; on sixth count, hop and kick both heels backward. Repeat.
   d. Camel walk. Stand with feet slightly apart. Place hands flat on the floor in front of feet. Keep elbows and knees straight. Walk forward moving right hand and leg simultaneously.
   e. Puppy dog walk. Assume position of a dog on all fours, with hands shoulder width apart. Walk, keeping arms and legs stiff.
   f. Stoop-stand. Place hands on hips and do deep knee bending.
   g. Crab walk. Take squat position. Place hands flat on floor in back of feet. Keep head, neck, and body in straight line and back toward the floor. Walk or run on hands and feet.

Figure 6–11. Crab Walk

3. **Exercises for Development of Abdominal Muscles**
   a. Rowboat. Two children sit cross-legged, facing each other and holding hands. One child leans backward pulling the other child. The order is reversed.
   b. Lying-to-sitting positions. Lie on back with arms outstretched over head; slowly raise body and touch toes without lifting feet from floor.
   c. Chinese getup. Two children, sitting back to back with elbows locked, attempt to gain a standing position by pushing against each other.

4. **Exercises for Improving Balance**
   a. Tightrope walk. Walk on a line drawn on the floor or on a crack, using arms for balance. The distance of the line should be 10 to 12 feet.

b. Airplane dip. Raise arms sideward; standing on one foot, extend other leg backward and bend body forward.

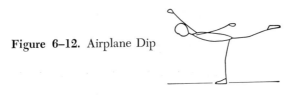

Figure 6–12. Airplane Dip

c. One-leg stand. Place hands on hips; stand on one foot, the other leg raised forward or backward with knee straight.
d. Backward jump. Stand with feet slightly apart. Jump backward without losing balance.

SUMMARY

Because growth and development are gradual processes, the teacher of seven- and eight-year-old children should be ever-conscious of the fact that they, like five- and six-year-olds, must be given opportunity to rest and relax. Their attention span is longer, and their interest span more sustained, but they must be guarded against overexertion.

A well-planned physical education program for these children provides opportunity to develop stronger muscles, better balance, satisfactory coordination, and a sense of the aesthetic. Such a program has been suggested in the preceding pages. It has been planned to help these children recognize their own abilities, set standards, play cooperatively, compete fairly, and improve skills. Through a program such as the one suggested in this chapter, seven- and eight-year-olds can receive fundamental education to prepare them for the period of preadolescence which lies ahead.

QUESTIONS AND TOPICS FOR DISCUSSION

1. What important growth factors should the teacher of seven- and eight-year-old children consider?
2. How do the games suggested in this chapter contribute to the physical development of these children?

3. Describe the fundamental rhythmic patterns developed with this age group.

4. How does the program in stunts and self-testing activities contribute to the development of the individual?

SUGGESTED ACTIVITY UNIT

Develop an activity unit based on the circus. Rhythmic activities interpreting the acts of circus animals, clowns, and aerial performers may form the core. The unit may be enriched by a study of circus life and the effects that the circus in a town has on its people—especially the young people.

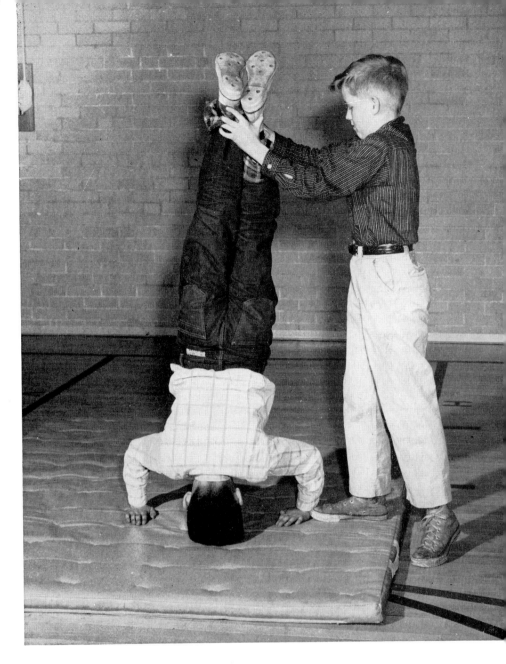

7. Program for the
Nine- and Ten-year-olds

Nine- and ten-year-old children are approaching or are in the preadolescent period. They are growing up; and it is necessary to think of them, not in terms of a certain age level, but in terms of their maturity level. There are such marked differences in interest levels among children of these ages that it is often difficult to work with them as a group.

Growth and Development. Physically, many of these children resemble their eight-year-old selves. Their growth pattern continues slowly. Girls develop more rapidly than boys during this period; however, growth for both boys and girls is uneven. Arms and legs seem unusually long, and hands and feet appear very large. The eyes, lungs, and heart, as well as the digestive and circulatory systems, are now almost mature. The heart, however, is especially subject to strain during this period of growth. Teeth may need straightening now, as the first and second bicuspids are appearing. Hand-eye coordination has greatly improved, as has muscle coordination. The children begin to show good balance of strength and growth and are interested in their own strength and skill in physical activities. They work and play hard. They will continue one activity—running, sliding, or playing ball—until exhausted, and they are also keenly interested in different types of team games.

Socially and emotionally, nine- and ten-year-old children progress at very different rates. They become more independent, cooperative, and dependable, but they are not consistent in these characteristics. Today they may be models of good behavior and tomorrow they may present a series of problems. The range in their maturity levels often causes group discipine problems. If a teacher hopes to avoid discipline problems with these children, he must forget that his children are all in the same age group and be ever-

140

conscious of the fact that there are many maturity levels within his group of nine- and ten-year-olds.

Most of these children respond well to praise and enjoy humor. They repeat again and again something that strikes them funny. They begin to accept jokes about themselves. They are aggressive and critical. The boys fight among themselves but make up readily. They enjoy competition. Interested in clubs and gangs, they not only form such groups with many friends but also pair off in close friendships. Usually the boys do not want to play with girls; it is at this age level that much teasing and antagonism between boys and girls appear.

These children worry about school and responsibilities. They need reassurance as to their ability. Intellectually they are maturing rapidly. They are beginning to think critically and develop a consciousness of the world about them. They show more interest in study and more ability to organize their thoughts. They utilize dictionaries and reference materials. They are capable of more analytical self-appraisal.

The Needs of These Children. Nine- and ten-year-olds need active, rough-and-tumble play. They need training in skills, but not too much pressure. They need reasonable explanations. Adults who get along with them do not "talk down" to them. These children need to know that their teacher likes them and that they have friends. To meet the needs of the children who are maturing at an average rate and of those who are maturing more slowly or more rapidly than the average rate, a program must be skillfully planned. A well-balanced program should include games, rhythms, dances, and self-testing activities.

In previous chapters, activity units illustrate the enrichment of a school's over-all program of work through an integration of physical education with other school subjects. In these chapters, physical education forms the center of interest for the units described. The motivation that initiates the activity is in each case a desire to learn to do something. The motivation for the following unit is intellectual rather than physical, but physical education supplements the other activities and adds zest and enjoyment to the unit as a whole.

A Class-planned Unit. A fifth-grade class had been studying the westward expansion of the United States. They had chosen as a caption for their unit "Builders of Our Country." The core of this unit was social studies. The class divided itself into groups to study how the explorers, pioneers, early settlers, Indians, cowboys, pony express riders, statesmen, scientists, and inventors all contributed to the building of America. They decided that every person who had ever lived in the United States and everyone who is now living here is a builder of America. They shared with one another the information they found in books. They prepared oral reports for presentation to another class and made pictures and scenes to illustrate their reports. Some of them made illustrated booklets of information.

They learned in their reading that the early builders of America liked to sing and dance and have fun just as we do, so they decided to prepare songs and dances that might have been enjoyed by the different builders of America. The "explorers" learned the song "In Fourteen Hundred Ninety-two;" the "Indians" sang "Poor Gitchi Manito" and danced a prayer dance; the "statesmen" and "scientists" sang "Wise Ben Franklin" and danced the minuet. "O Susannah" and "Old Brass Wagon" were chosen by the "pioneers" as their singing dances, and the "cowboys" sang "Goodbye Old Paint" and danced "Put Your Little Foot." "The Irish Lilt" and "Czebogar" were the dances of the "immigrants," who had learned folk songs of several countries. Thus physical education was used to supplement a unit of work which provided for the several interest and maturity levels found in an average class of nine- and ten-year-old children.

The unit plan of instruction is especially successful with this age group because their interest and attention spans have greatly increased. They have patience and persistence that children in the younger age groups do not possess. If their initial interest in an activity is keen enough, they will work day after day to perfect their skill in it.

One fifth-grade group had discussed the conditioning necessary for athletes. The subject of rope jumping as a conditioner was introduced. Thinking that the children might enjoy the experience of jumping rope to the accompaniment of rhythm records, the teacher distributed ropes to the class. The teacher, as well as the children, soon learned that jumping rope is a definite skill—one that most girls acquire easily but that some boys find difficult. They also discovered, however, that jumping to the accompaniment of music is sometimes difficult even for girls.

The boys and girls experienced such failure that the teacher thought they would be discouraged and give up. Instead of giving up, the boys asked if they might watch the girls jump without the music. When the girls needed a rest, the teacher played one of the records, and they all clapped the beat of the music. Next the girls tried jumping with ropes while the record played. They were much more successful than they had been at the beginning of the period. When the period ended, they did not want to leave the gymnasium. They boys asked to try "just once more" and, though it was time to go home, they tried once more.

The next day six boys came to school with ropes of their own. Their interest in learning to jump rope was so keen that they practiced both on the playground and at home, with help from some of the girls. They were all eager for physical education time and did not understand why their class could not use the gymnasium during their gym period each day, why the gymnasium schedule couldn't be rearranged while they were learning this skill.

When the teacher convinced them that every group scheduled for the gymnasium had skills to learn too, they convinced the teacher that they could jump in their classroom without disturbing other classes. While they were practicing consideration for the teacher and children whose room was underneath theirs, they were also gaining skill in both light and rhythmic jumping. When they had really mastered the skill, it was interesting to note that the children were ready for a different activity. They were always ready to demonstrate their skill, but the eagerness evident during their practice periods was lacking.

With children of this age, a wise teacher alters his own plans if the whole group develops a keen interest in some activity the teacher had not considered of major importance. These children need the feeling of satisfaction that comes with success in attaining a goal set by themselves. An activity is worthwhile when the children have had so much enjoyment from participation that they spontaneously say, "Let's do it again!"

The physical education program must provide games and activities that satisfy children's interest in competition and develop skills to a degree which fulfills their growing desire for perfection. The program must include large-group games and team games. The latter type of game appeals to the club and gang spirit evident in these children. Physical education for this group must provide activities which require self-testing of strength, muscular development, and skill improvement. It must refine old skills and teach new skills that improve muscle and eye-hand coordination. Throwing and catching a ball, walking, running, skipping, hopping, jumping, and swinging provide means for improving muscle coordination. In order to prevent overfatigue, the physical education program for this group should include methods of checking the energy expended with each activity, for it must be remembered that the heart of the child in this group is especially subject to strain. The program should also include games attractive to each sex, as well as those enjoyed by both sexes. It should include many team games—games with definite but simple rules which help children solve their own problems as they arise. Games with complicated rules result in too much arguing among the players and require too much mediation by the teacher.

GAMES

Outdoor—Large-group Games

A. Pom Pom Pullaway
1. *Purpose*
   a. To react quickly
   b. To wait for a signal
   c. To run fast
   d. To avoid being tagged
2. *Equipment*
   None
3. *Description*
   Two parallel lines are drawn, about 35 feet apart. Children

stand side by side, holding hands. One child is selected to stand between the lines. The first child in the line squeezes the hand he is holding, and each child passes the squeeze down the line. As soon as the last child's hand is squeezed, he calls out, "Pom pom pullaway." This is the signal for hands to be dropped and for all to run to the other line. Any child tagged by the child in the middle remains with him in the middle and helps tag others. The last child to be tagged wins the game.

B. Red Rover

1. *Purpose*
   a. To learn to wait for a signal
   b. To move fast
2. *Equipment*
   None
3. *Description*
   Two parallel lines are drawn on the playground, about 35 feet apart. The class is divided into two groups. The teams stand beyond the boundary lines, one team on each side. The player chosen to be "it" calls out, "Red Rover, Red Rover, come on over here." Players on each side exchange places. Any player tagged by "it" remains with him to help him tag other players. The last player tagged wins.

C. Overtake

1. *Purpose*
   To learn to receive and pass a ball quickly
2. *Equipment*
   Two volleyballs, basketballs, or large rubber balls
3. *Description*
   Class stands in a single-circle formation, facing center. One ball is given to a player on one side of the circle, and the other ball to a player on opposite side of the circle. At a signal, the players pass the balls to their left as rapidly as possible, until the second ball overtakes the first. A player who drops the ball must recover it himself.

D. Spud

1. *Purpose*
   a. To learn to be alert

b. To learn to throw and catch a ball

c. To learn to dodge

2. *Equipment*

6-inch rubber ball

3. *Description*

Number of players—fifteen to thirty. The class is grouped around a leader, who holds the ball. The leader whispers a number from one to thirty in each child's ear. The leader then throws the ball straight up in the air, calling out a number as he does so. The instant the ball leaves the leader's hand, the group scatters, until the child whose number has been called catches the ball and shouts, "Spud!" All the children stop running immediately and stand where they are while the child takes aim and tries to hit one of the children with the ball. A child may duck when he sees the ball coming but may not move his feet while doing so. If the child is hit with the ball, he gets the letter S and becomes the leader, and the play resumes. When a child gets all the letters S P U D, he is out of the game. The winner is the child with the fewest letters at the end of a time period agreed upon before the game.

Indoor—Large-group Games

A. Automobile Relay

1. *Purpose*

a. To learn to follow directions

b. To learn to respond quickly to a signal

c. To learn to run swiftly

2. *Equipment*

None

3. *Description*

At a given signal, the first child in each alternate row leaves his seat on the right, encircles the row, and returns to his seat. As soon as the first child is seated, the second child leaves his seat on the right, completely encircles his row, and returns to his seat. The winning row is the one whose last player is seated first. The remaining alternate rows then play. The winning row of this group competes with the winners of the first group.

B. Hand-over-head Beanbag
   1. *Purpose*
       a. To learn to take turns
       b. To learn to follow directions accurately
   2. *Equipment*
       One beanbag for each row
   3. *Description*
       Each row has an even number of players. Children sit in their seats, and one beanbag is placed on the first desk in each row. On a given signal, the first player in each row picks up the beanbag, raises his hand over his head, and drops, not throws, the beanbag on the desk behind him. The second player catches or picks up the beanbag and in like manner drops the beanbag on the desk behind him. When the last player picks up the beanbag, he runs directly to the front of his row, and everyone in the row moves back one seat. The last player takes the first seat and starts the beanbag again down the row. This continues until the first player in the row returns to his seat. The winning row is the one whose leader returns first to his seat, holds the beanbag high, and announces that his row has finished.

C. Schoolroom Dodge Ball
   1. *Purpose*
       a. To learn to dodge
       b. To learn to throw accurately
   2. *Equipment*
       6-inch rubber ball
   3. *Description*
       The children form a circle, standing informally in front of the room or in the aisles. The leader tosses the ball into the group, trying to hit someone. The children dodge to avoid being hit. Anyone hit by the ball is eliminated from the game. After four players have been eliminated, the first one returns; no more than four are out of the game at one time. A child is chosen to pick up the ball and toss it into

the group. This child chooses another, and so on until all have had a turn.

Fouls: (*a*) To sit or lie on the floor while dodging; (*b*) to sit in a chair while dodging.

D. Follow-the-leader

1. *Purpose*
   a. To observe accurately
   b. To react quickly to the leader's directions
2. *Equipment*
   None
3. *Description*
   The children form a line behind a leader, who moves about the room performing various stunts. Each child must imitate the leader, who does such stunts as skipping, hopping, walking stiff-legged, jumping over low obstacles, and reaching.

   Fouls: (*a*) Failing to follow leader accurately; (*b*) failing to change from one stunt to another immediately.

E. Numbers Change

1. *Purpose*
   To respond quickly to a signal
2. *Equipment*
   None
3. *Description*
   Players stand in a circle, facing the center. One child is "it" and stands in the center. The children forming the circle are numbered consecutively. "It" calls any two numbers in the circle, and the two children with those numbers try to exchange places before "it" moves into one or the other's place. The one who is left out of the circle becomes "it."

Outdoor—Small-group Games and Races

A. Touch Relay

1. *Purpose*
   To learn to react quickly to leader's directions
2. *Equipment*
   None

3. *Description*

The players line up on a starting line in two rows, an equal number of players in each row. The leader stands out in front of one group and names some object in view of the players. As soon as the object is named, the players run, touch the object, and return to position. The first line with all its players in position scores a point. The leader usually names indefinite objects, such as wood, iron, something black, etc. However, he may name a specific object. The game is more fun if the leader also tells the players what to do when they return to position—for example, touch wood and come back and stand on right foot.

B. Tunnel Relay

1. *Purpose*

a. To increase skill in rolling a ball

b. To develop speed in moving

2. *Equipment*

An 8-inch rubber ball for each team

3. *Description*

The teams line up, with the leaders standing on the starting line. Each leader holds a ball until the signal to begin is given. Then the ball is rolled down between the legs of the players. If the ball goes out of the line, it is recovered by the player in front of whom it left the line. From his position, this player restarts the ball. When the last player in line gets the ball, he runs forward to the starting line, where he again puts the ball in play. The winning team is the one which first succeeds in getting back into starting position.

C. One Old Cat

1. *Purpose*

a. To increase skill in batting, throwing, and catching

b. To run bases swiftly

2. *Equipment*

Bat, softball, two bases

3. *Description*

Three or more children may play this game. One base is home plate, and the other, which is placed about 30 feet from home plate, is first base. One child is the pitcher; he throws the ball to the catcher, 35 feet away. The batter tries to hit the ball as it passes. If he misses and the catcher catches it before it hits the ground, or on the first bound, the batter is out. Then the catcher goes to bat, the pitcher becomes catcher, and the batter is pitcher. If the batter hits the ball, he tries to run to first base and return home before the ball can be fielded to either the catcher or the pitcher to hold while touching home plate. If the batter succeeds in making the round trip, he scores one run and continues at bat until he is put out. The winning player is the one with the highest number of runs. If more than three children play, they are numbered and take turns being batter.

D. Wheel Tag
1. *Purpose*
   a. To learn to follow directions
   b. To increase speed in running
2. *Equipment*
   None
3. *Description*
   The children form a circle that is four deep. One child, who is "it," runs around the outside of the circle and tags the rear, or number 4 player in any line. Number 4 tags number 3, who tags number 2; number 2 tags number 1, who chases the child who is "it." If "it" can tag another number 4 before he is tagged, the new number 1 becomes the chaser. "It" becomes number 4.

Indoor—Small-group Games

A. Paddle Ball
1. *Purpose*
   a. To improve the skill of volleying a sponge or badminton bird over a net
   b. To learn to keep score
2. *Equipment*
   A rope or volleyball net stretched between two jump stand-

ards; wooden paddles; small pieces of sponge or badminton bird

3. *Description*

Standards are placed 15 feet apart. A rope or net is placed at a height of 3 feet. Two players stand at either side of the net. The player at the right of one team serves the sponge or bird across the net to the player diagonally opposite on the other team. All players try to keep the rubber sponge in the air by batting it back and forth across the net.

Scoring: One point is scored for the serving side each time the opponents fail to keep the sponge in the air. Score as in volleyball or tennis.

B. Roly Poly

1. *Purpose*

   a. To learn to keep score

   b. To learn to roll a ball through a target

2. *Equipment*

   Three sponge-rubber balls, a roly-poly board

3. *Description* (see Figure 7–1)

   The roly-poly board is set up at an end of an aisle near a wall. A starting line is drawn about 12 feet from the board. Each child rolls three balls, one at a time, attempting to put them through the holes in the roly-poly board.

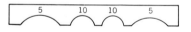

Figure 7–1. Roly Poly

Scoring: Players receive 5 points for each ball that goes through the large opening, 10 points for those that go through small openings.

C. Ring Toss

1. *Purpose*

   a. To learn to take turns

   b. To improve skill in tossing an object at a target

2. *Equipment*
Six rope rings; two wooden stakes on small platforms, stakes about 8 inches high

3. *Description*
Stakes are placed about 10 feet apart. Two children, standing by one stake, take turns tossing three rings at the other stake. The same children go to the second stake, score their ringers, and pitch the three rings back to the first stake. Another pair of children take their turns.
Scoring: Each ringer counts 1 point.

Team Games

A. Softball

1. *Purpose*
   a. To become acquainted with the rules of softball and baseball
   b. To improve the skill of batting a ball
   c. To improve the skill of throwing and catching a ball
   d. To learn to run bases swiftly

2. *Equipment*
Softball, bats, bases

3. *Description*
Two teams of nine or ten players each are chosen. One team take their places in the field, as designated in the diagram (see Figure 7–2). The pitcher pitches the ball underhand to the batter, who attempts to hit the ball into fair territory. If the pitcher pitches four balls that are not over the plate, the batter may go to first base. A batter is out if he has three strikes or if he hits a fly ball which is caught by any member of the opposing team. A base runner is out if he is tagged by any opponent with the ball or if he is forced to run to a base where an opponent has the ball. When the team at bat has three outs, it is retired and the opposing team takes its turn at bat.
Fouls: (a) A ball is foul if it is hit anywhere outside the base lines; (b) a foul is called a strike unless it would be the third strike; (c) the third strike must be a swinging strike or a called one.

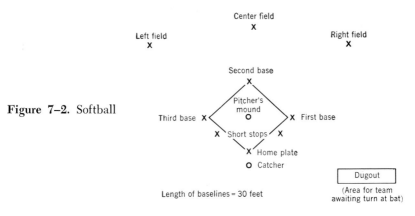

Center field
X

Left field
X

Right field
X

Second base
X

Figure 7–2. Softball

Pitcher's
mound
Third base X   O   X First base

X `Short stops` X

X Home plate

O Catcher

Dugout

Length of baselines = 30 feet

(Area for team
awaiting turn at bat)

B. Corner Ball

1. *Purpose*
    a. To throw ball over the heads of the opposing team to
    the corner man
    b. To improve skill in throwing a ball accurately
2. *Equipment*
   A volleyball
3. *Description* (see Figure 7–3)
   The playing area is divided into halves, and a 6-foot square
   is marked off in each corner. The class is divided into two
   teams. Each team takes one-half the playing area. Each
   team places two of its players in the corners of the opponent's court. These players must not step outside their goal
   squares. The ball is tossed to see which team starts first.
   The referee tosses the ball in from the side to a player in
   the forward line of the team winning the toss. The player
   who catches the ball attempts to throw it to one of his

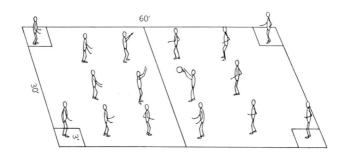

Figure 7–3.
Corner Ball

60'

30'

3'

corner men, but he may not walk or run with it. When the ball is in play, no player may step over the center line or hold the ball more than three seconds. When a corner man catches the ball, he returns it to a player on the opposing team. It is illegal for a player to step into his opponent's goal.

Scoring: One point is scored whenever a baseman catches a ball thrown by a member of his team.

Fouls: Whenever a player breaks any of the rules listed above, a foul is called, and the ball is given to the other team.

C. Outdoor Volleyball

1. *Purpose*

   a. To improve skill in batting ball over a net

   b. To improve balance

2. *Equipment*

   A regulation volleyball, a net, two posts, a rectangular playing area, 30 by 60 feet

3. *Description* (see Figure 7–4)

   The net is stretched 7 feet 6 inches high across posts which are placed 1 foot outside the side line. The net divides the court into two equal playing areas. The ball is put into play by means of a service and is kept in the air by volleying. One point is earned by the side serving the ball when the opposing team fails to return the ball to the opponent's court. The ball is dead when it touches the ground. A dead ball is returned to the opponent's team for service. A player must not catch or hold the ball; however, a player may volley the ball twice if necessary. (The official volleyball rules do not permit this.)

   Number of players: Any number divided into two equal sides. Number 1 is the first server. After the service, players rotate according to the arrow.

   Serving: The server holds the ball in his left hand and hits it with the open palm of his right hand. The server remains the same until the side loses the ball. The ball goes to the opposing team when the serving team fails to keep the ball from touching the ground or fouls in any other way. The team that is on the side that first reaches the score of 21 points wins.

Fouls: (*a*) Touching the net with the body; (*b*) hitting the ball more than two times; (*c*) crossing the center line; (*d*) catching or holding the ball; (*e*) stepping over the line when serving.

Note: If children are not strong enough to volley the ball, they may play the game at first by throwing and catching the ball.

Figure 7–4. Volleyball

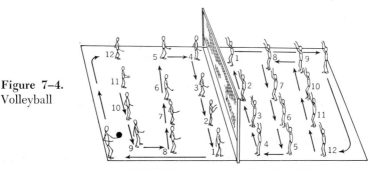

Net 7'6" high across posts placed 1' outside side lines
Court 30' × 60'

D. Soccer Baseball

1. *Purpose*
   a. To learn to kick the ball accurately
   b. To improve skill in catching a ball
   c. To improve skill in throwing a ball
   d. To acquaint children with rules of baseball
2. *Equipment*
   A soccer ball, large playing area
3. *Description*
   Bases are placed 15 to 30 feet part, and the pitcher's box is placed 20 to 30 feet from home plate. The general rules of baseball are used in soccer baseball, with these exceptions:
   a. The ball is kicked instead of batted.
   b. No bunting is allowed.

      c. There can be no stealing of bases or running on a passed ball.

      d. Sliding to bases is against the rules.

      e. Three fouls put a kicker out. The base runner may be "thrown out," that is, if the base is tagged with the ball, or touched by a baseman or fielder who has the ball in his hands, before the runner reaches base.

      f. A kicker must keep one foot on home base while kicking. An out is made if the kicker runs up on the ball. The pitcher bowls the ball to the kicker, who kicks the ball into the field and runs to first base.

E. Schoolroom Volleyball

  1. *Purpose*

      a. To learn to keep score

      b. To learn the rules of the game

      c. To improve volleyball skills

  2. *Equipment*

    A large rubber ball, light-weight beach ball, or inflated bladder with air tube taped against the side.

  3. *Description*

    The class is divided into two teams. The teams face each other, and the center aisle serves as a net. The child in the rear right corner starts the game by serving the ball. The regular rules of volleyball are followed (see page 154).

    Scoring: The serving team scores (*a*) each time the ball touches the floor on the opponent's side of the center aisle; (*b*) each time the ball is touched last by a child on the opposing team before it goes out of bounds.

F. Schoolroom Newcomb

  1. *Purpose*

      a. To learn to throw an object accurately

      b. To learn to catch skillfully

  2. *Equipment*

    A 5-inch rubber ball or beanbag

  3. *Description*

    The class is divided into two teams. The children stand in aisles, facing the opposing team. The center row of seats represents the dividing line. Four children, one for each corner of the room, are selected, and it is their duty to protect the sides of the room and to keep the ball in play. The ball is given to a player, who starts the game by trying to throw the ball so that it touches the floor on the other side of the dividing line. The players of the opposing team try to prevent the ball from touching the floor on their side of the line. The person catching the ball may throw it back over the net or pass it to another member of his team to throw. If the ball falls short of the dividing line, the player nearest the place where the ball rolls picks it up and starts the play again. When the ball rolls outside the play area, the nearest player gets it and throws it to a member of his team from the point where it had originally left the field of play.

Fouls: (*a*) Taking more than one step while holding the ball; (*b*) touching the dividing line or net.

Scoring: One point is scored whenever the ball touches the floor on the opponent's side of the dividing line, provided it is propelled there by a player standing on the other side of the dividing line. The first team scoring 15 points wins. After 5 points are scored, players should rotate. Children standing in the aisles next to the dividing line move to the last aisle. Each row moves up one aisle.

RHYTHMS AND DANCE

The more advanced patterns of music to which nine- and ten-year old children are capable of responding require an extension of the rhythmic experiences based on fundamental rhythmic patterns. The children of this age group should review and become more familiar with basic musical patterns, and they should be encouraged to be creative in adapting their movements to dance patterns. By extending the activities of walking, running, skipping, and jumping to include variations and combinations of these natural patterns, children gain confidence and ability in rhythmic response. Combinations of walking and bowing, running and turning, sliding and bending, twisting and swaying give children experience in adapting these patterns of movement to basic dance steps. The ability and interest levels of the group determine for the teacher the type of dance program to be taught.

By continuing to adapt rhythmic patterns to simple folk dances and singing games, children learn to respond gracefully. Participation in such activity results in improvement in bodily movement and in enjoyment of social activity. In learning singing games, children should become familiar with the words and music before attempting to combine the steps with the words. At the beginning, the class may be divided into two groups, one to sing and the other to dance. As soon as the children are familiar with the dance and song, all should participate.

In teaching folk dances, the objectives are to foster the children's enjoyment and to develop their ability to respond to music. Therefore, the teacher should carefully select dances which the group can learn successfully. The dances and singing games suggested here appeal to the interest and ability of nine- and ten-year-olds. Music for these activities will be found in the Appendix. Recordings are listed at the end of Part Two, pages 218 and 219.

Dance Steps

POLKA

This is one of the fast-moving steps used in folk dancing. "Run, run, run, hop" describes the step, which is done to 2/4 music.

Step Analysis

———— ————   ———— ———— Underlying beat

—— —— ——. ——   —— ——   —— —— Foot pattern
R   L   R   R   L   R   L   L

In polka music, two counts underlie each measure. Two movements are executed on each count, making the step a very fast one.

Formation for Practice. The children join hands and form a large circle. Starting clockwise, they slide sixteen slides in the line of direction, still facing the center of the circle. Without stopping, they slide sixteen slides counterclockwise; then eight slides clockwise, eight slides counterclockwise; four slides clockwise, four slides counterclockwise; two slides clockwise, two slides counterclockwise; two slides clockwise and two counterclockwise.

From this progression, the children face clockwise around the room. In this formation, without changing direction, they take the sixteen-sixteen, eight-eight, four-four, two-two, and two-two combinations, advancing around the circle. Dancers start with the right foot and alternate leads for each change.

The two-two combination is the polka step. When children master the previous progressions, they may try the two-two combination, or polka step, alone, advancing around the room.

Face-to-face and Back-to-back Polka. In partner formation, with inside hands joined, children start with outside feet. The first polka step is taken with partners facing each other, swinging their joined arms back; they continue advancing around the room, taking the next step back to back and swinging their arms forward. Many folk dances use this step.

Waist-shoulder Position. The boy places his hands on his partner's waist, and the girl places her hands on her partner's shoulders. The boy starts with his left foot, and the girl starts with her right foot. In this position, the step may be done moving forward, backward, or in a spiral direction.

WALTZ

An even 3/4 beat characterizes the waltz step. Often confused with the two-step (step, close, step), the waltz (step, step, close), is one of the simplest dance steps and yet one of the most difficult to master. This basic dance step is included in many folk dances and in ballroom dancing.

Step Analysis

— — — — — — — — — — — — Underlying beat

— — — — — — — — — — — — Foot pattern

R L R   L R L   R L R   L R L

(close)   (close)   (close)   (close)

Each step is taken directly forward, backward, or to the side.

Box, or Square Waltz. Dancers step directly forward left, step to the side right, close left to right. To start the second half of the box, or square, they step back right, step side left, close right to left. When dancing in social dance position, boys start the box waltz by stepping forward left and girls step directly back right. In a very limited space, this formation permits the dancer to concentrate on moving with the music while actually covering only a small area.

Formation for Practice. The waltz step is often learned more easily if children are grouped informally, though all should face the same direction. The teacher may either face the class or stand with her back to the children. The waltz step should be practiced individually at first. When the class masters the step moving forward and backward, the girls turn to face the boys, taking the step in reverse of the boys. This is the position they use in the dance. Then they should try the step in the elbow position: boys hold girls' arms at the elbows, and girls place their hands on the boys' forearms. Using the elbow position before the social dancing position often gives the boys and girls more confidence until they master the foot pattern.

A similar progression may be used in teaching the box waltz—individually, all facing in the same direction; individually, boys and girls facing; elbow position in partners; and social dance position in partners.

TWO-STEP

The "step, together, step, hold" of the two-step, done to 2/4 music, is often danced for a waltz. It is a fast step and approaches the skip when done rapidly.

Step Analysis

——— —— ——— —— ——— —— ——— —— Underlying beat

— — — — — — — — — — — — Foot pattern

R L R L R L R L R L R L

Dancers step right, close left to right, step right and hold; step left, close right to left, step left and hold. The step may be danced to either side, forward, backward, or on a turn.

Formation for Practice. The children are arranged in lines facing the teacher. They step to the side right, close left to right, step right and hold; step to left, close right to left and hold. Forgetting the hold often causes the dancer trouble. The weight does not change to the other foot on the hold. When the step is mastered to the side, the children may try advancing and moving backward. Girls can then turn and face the boys, practicing the boys' movements in reverse. After the individual practice, partners should try the different combinations in the elbow position before going on to the social dance position.

SCHOTTISCHE

"Step, step, step, hop" describes the schottische. The combination of a schottische step with step-hops makes this an interesting dance step. Boys and girls like to develop different combinations of their own—usually two schottische steps with four step-hops. The step is taken to 4/4 music.

Step Analysis

— — — —   — — — —   — — — —   — — — — Underlying
                                                             beat

— — — —   — — — —   — — — —   — — — — Foot
                                                             pattern

R L R R   L R L L   R L R R   L R L L
   (hop)   (hop)   (hop)   (hop)

Formation for Practice. The skaters' position (partners clasp right hands and left hands, right hands on top) is a good one for learning the schottische step and may be used when combining two schottische steps with four step-hops.

Folk Dancing

BEAN SETTING

Parts of the Music
A, two phrases (measures 1 to 4, 5 to 8); B, two phrases (measures 9 to 12, 13 to 16); the music should be repeated four times
Rhythmic Pattern
6/8 time, counted two beats to each measure
Step
Morris—a step, then a hop on the same foot, the free foot extended forward with the leg straight

Position

Three couples form a set, one couple behind another. A stick about the thickness of a broom handle and not more than 18 inches long is grasped in the center with the right hand and carried shoulder high by each member of the set.

The Dance

1. The music plays through once while all stand facing the head of the set with sticks crossed and held about shoulder high. Each dancer strikes his partner's stick on the last beat.

2. Ring: All form a circle facing clockwise in the set. They circle in this direction on phrase one of part A of the music, using eight Morris steps. On phrase two, dancers return to their places, finishing in beginning position, one couple behind another.

   Dib and strike: To dib is to hold the stick by the center and strike it against the floor, then lift it up. On the first count of part B, dancers dib with the bottom of the stick; on the second count, they dib with the top of the stick; on the third count, partners strike their sticks together, and on count 4, they hold. All dib with the bottom of the stick; then with top of the stick; and pass the strike around the set —1 strikes 3's stick; 3 strikes 5's stick; 5 strikes 6's stick; 6 strikes 4's stick; 4 strikes 2's stick; 2 strikes 1's stick; partners strike each other's sticks on the last count.

3. Crossover: Partners face each other, and all three couples exchange places with the Morris step, using four steps across and four to turn around facing back. On the second phrase of part A, partners return to place, passing left shoulders.

   Dib and strike.

4. Back to back: Partners move forward passing to the left; without turning around, they back up and return to place.

   Dib and strike.

5. Hey: Using the Morris step, each dancer makes a figure 8, with all dancers moving at the same time and each line forming a figure 8. The head couple faces down the set, and the other two couples face the head of the set (see diagram).

1 and 2 start on the first count of part A; the others wait until the third count to start. Dancers 1, 2, 3, and 4 start out to their left, and 5 and 6 start to their right. At the end of the first phrase, the dancers should be halfway through their 8; it is necessary to gauge the size of the steps in order to finish with the music.

Dib and strike.

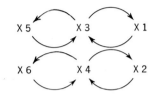

Starting position for the *Hey;* arrows indicate directions for moving.

LITTLE MAN IN A FIX

Parts of the Music

A, two phrases (measures 1 to 4, 5 to 8), repeated; B, two phrases (measures 9 to 12, 13 to 16), repeated

Rhythmic Pattern

3/4 time, three counts to each measure

Steps

Running step, kicking feet forward; hopsa waltz—step, hop, hop

Position

Sets of two couples, each in a line of four. Girl places left hand on partner's right shoulder, and boy places right arm around partner's waist. Boys link left arms so that couples face in reverse directions.

The Dance

1. To part A of the music, all take running step, kicking feet forward as they circle in sets of four in wheel position.

   Boys join left hands forming an arch. Girls run forward under the arch, each holding her partner's hand with her left hand. Girls turn and join right hands, making a small wheel. Leaning away from the center, all run clockwise in this small circle.

   Dancers finish with partners facing, both hands joined and arms extended shoulder high.

2. To part B, couples do a hopsa waltz, turning and progressing around the room.

   Each couple selects another couple for the next dance.

SELLENGER'S ROUND

Rhythmic Pattern
6/8 time counted two beats to each measure
Steps
Running step, walking step, sliding step
Position
Single circle, partners facing center with hands joined
The Dance

1. Eight slides to the right around circle; eight slides to the left around circle. To part A of the music.
2. "Side right with partners." With four walking steps, partners change places, passing to the right. To part B, measures 1 and 2.
3. "Turn single." With four running steps, partners turn around to right in place. To part B, measures 3 and 4.
4. Partners repeat 2 and 3 to the left. To part B, measures 5 to 8.
5. "Arm right with partners." Partners link right arms and swing, taking four running steps. To part B, repeat measures 1 and 2.
6. 3, 5, and 3 are repeated. To part B, measures 3 to 8.

COME, LET US BE JOYFUL

Verse

> Come, let us be joyful
> While life is happy and gay,
> Gathering roses
> All along the way.

Chorus

> We're always making our lives so blue;
> We look for thorns and we find them too,
> And leave the violets quite unseen
> That on our way do grow.

Parts of the Music
A, two phrases; B, two phrases (A repeated after B)
Rhythmic Pattern
6/8 time, counted two beats to each measure

Steps
  Walking step, skipping step
Position
  Sets of three, a boy in the center and a girl on either side, facing another set of three. These sets of six form a large circle around the room. The center dancer joins hands with the outside dancers.
The Dance
  1. On phrase 1 of part A of the music, the two lines of three advance toward each other with three walking steps, bow, and return to place. On phrase 2, repeat.
  2. On phrase 1 of part B, the center person links right elbows with the girl on his right and turns with four skipping steps. He then links left elbows with the girl on the left and turns her. While these dancers turn, the free dancer continues skipping and moves out to the side, describing a loop clockwise; he returns just in time to hook elbows with the center dancer. On phrase 2, repeat.
  3. On phrase 1 of part A, dancers advance and return as in 1, but do not repeat.
     On phrase 2, dancers advance, releasing hands; they continue ahead, passing right shoulders with the person directly across, meet a new set of three, and repeat the whole dance.

CSEBOGAR

Rhythmic Pattern
  2/4 time
Steps
  Walking step, skipping step, sliding step
Position
  Single circle, hands joined, partners side by side
The Dance
  1. To the first part of the music, all circle to the right with eight slides. This is repeated to the left. Dancers walk four steps to center, return to place with four steps back. Partners stand with right sides together, right arm around partner's

waist and left hand held high. Partners skip around each other.

2. For the second part of the music, partners face, hands joined and arms at shoulder height. They do four steps back, two slides; four slides to center of circle, four back to place; two slides to center, two slides back to place. Left arm held high, right arm around partner's waist, partners skip around each other.

Repeat.

MINUET

Rhythmic Pattern

3/4 time, counted six to each two measures

Steps

Step and point, crossover step, pirouette, balance step

Position

Partners face forward, inside hands joined. Girls hold skirts with outside hands. They begin with the outside foot. Partner on right follows the directions given below. Partner on left uses reverse foot throughout the dance.

The Dance

1. Step forward obliquely to the right (count 1); bring left foot to right (count 2); step right obliquely (count 3); point left toe obliquely forward (count 4) and hold for counts 5 and 6.

   Repeat twice.

   Crossover step to change places with partner—step sideways to the left (counts 1 and 2); draw right foot to left (count 3); step sideways to left (count 4).

   Pirouette—cross right toe behind, close to left heel, and turn a three-quarter circle left, ending facing partner (counts 5 and 6). In doing the pirouette, the dancers are high on their toes.

2. Join right hands with partner. Balance step—step forward left (count 1); bring right foot up to left, raising both heels (count 2); lower heels (count 3).

   Repeat stepping backward to right.

Repeat left and right—four balance steps in all.

Walk six short steps in a half circle, beginning with left foot and changing places with partner.

Now the original right partner is at right again. Bow, step sideways to the left (count 1); swing right foot behind left, bend right knee to make a curtsy (count 2); straighten right knee, slowly rising (count 3); step left in place (count 4); step right sideways (count 5); bring left foot to right (count 6).

IRISH LILT

Rhythmic Pattern

6/8 time, counted four to each two measures

Steps

Hop, break

Position

Dancers standing in informal groups facing in the same direction, hands on hips

The Dance

1. Raising left foot backward, hop on right foot; then hop on left foot, raising right foot forward. Repeat in the same manner five times.

   "Break!" Jump, landing with feet astride (count 1); jump, landing with feet together (count 2); hop on left foot, raising right foot backward (count 3); hop on left foot, raising right foot forward (count 4).

   Repeat all.

2. Touch right toe forward four times while hopping four times on left foot.

   Repeat, hopping four times on right foot and touching left toe.

   Touch right toe forward two times while hopping two times on left foot.

   Repeat, hopping two times on right foot, touching left toe forward.

   "Break" as in 1.

3. Touching right foot sideward with the toe inverted, heel up,

hop on left foot. Hop again on left foot, touching right foot sideways this time with heel down, toe up.

Repeat, hopping on right foot (one measure of music).

Repeat all twice more, hopping alternately on left, then right foot (four measures).

"Break!"

4. Cross right foot in front of left, stepping on it. Step on left, bring it close to right (count 1); repeat (count 2), moving to left (one measure).

Repeat (one measure).

Repeat all, crossing left foot over right and moving to right (two measures).

Repeat same step, crossing right over left (one measure).

Repeat, crossing left foot over right (one measure).

"Break!"

Complete the dance by repeating 1.

PUT YOUR LITTLE FOOT

Rhythmic Pattern

3/4 time

Position

In couples, as described below

The Dance

1. Boy at left of partner and slightly behind her, right hands joined at girl's right shoulder, boy's arm behind girl, left hands joined in front. Left foot is swung back across the right.

   a. Step left with left foot (count 1); bring right foot to left foot (count 2). Step left with left foot (count 3) and point right toe diagonally forward to right (counts 1, 2, 3).

   b. Starting with right foot, repeat *a.*

   c. Repeat *a* and *b.*

   In dancing these steps *a* through *c,* the boy takes short steps, the girl takes somewhat longer steps and crosses to the other side, each time in front of the boy. On count

3 of *c*, the dancers swing their left foot back across their right foot.

  d. Step left with left foot (count 1); bring right foot to left (count 2); step left with left foot (count 3); bring right foot to left foot (count 4); step left with left foot and point right toe diagonally forward to right (count 5).

  e. Starting with the right foot, repeat *d*.

  f. Repeat *d* and *e*.

2. Same as part 1, except for position. Partners take skating position for part 2.

  a. The girl turns in front of the boy, who dances in place. The girl finishes on left of the boy the first time; returns to her position on the boy's right the second time; to the left of the boy the third time; and to the right the fourth time.

  b. Boys and girls dance in their own positions.

3. Same as part 1, except for position. Partners take ballroom-dancing position for this part.

KOLO

Rhythmic Pattern

  2/4 time

Steps

  Running step

  Kolo—step right with right foot, cross left foot behind right, step right with right foot, hop

Position

  Dancers side by side in single lines, hands on each other's shoulders

The Dance

1. Introduction. Start with right foot, run four steps forward and four steps backward.

2. Step to right with right foot. Cross left foot behind right foot and step to right with right foot. Hop on right foot, raising left foot across in front of right foot. Repeat to left. Repeat to right and left.

3. Step right, hop on right foot, raising left foot across in front of right. Repeat on left foot.

Repeat to right and left.

4. Step right, cross left foot behind right. Repeat twice.

Step right, hop on right foot, raising left foot across in front of right.

Figure 7–5. Kolo

O SUSANNAH

Parts of the Music

Verse, two phrases, repeated; chorus, two phrases, repeated

Rhythmic Pattern

2/4 time

Steps

Walking step

Square-dance steps—a dragging run, with an occasional catch step if the dancer wishes (feet kept close to the floor, knees slightly bent to avoid bouncing)

Position

Single circle facing center, with partners side by side

The Dance

1. On phrase 1 of the verse, girls walk toward center of the circle three steps, salute, and return to place.

On phrase 2, boys walk to center of circle three steps, salute, and return to place.

2. On phrase 1 of the chorus, partners face, do a grand right and left, and take the seventh person in promenade position (skater's position with left hands joined and right hands joined on top of left).

On phrase 2, promenade counterclockwise around the circle.

3. Entire dance is repeated.

WEGGIS

Parts of the Music
Introduction, two measures; verse, two phrases; chorus, two phrases

Rhythmic Pattern
2/4 time

Steps
Heel-and-toe polka—touch left heel in front, touch left toe in back of right; polka step left; run left, run right; run left, hop left.

Step-hop—step left, hop left; step right, hop right.

Step and point toe diagonally forward.

The Dance
Verse 1. Heel-and-toe polka, starting left. Repeat three times.

Chorus. Face partner. Take one polka step away from partner, one polka step toward partner, and join both hands. Take four step-hops around partner. Repeat.

Verse 2. Step sideward left and point right toe across in front of left. Repeat to right. Repeat all.

Chorus. Repeat steps of first chorus.

Introduction. Honor partner.

Verse 3. Repeat steps of verse 2.

Chorus. Repeat steps of chorus, taking step-hops with new partner on the right.

HEEL-AND-TOE POLKA

Rhythmic Pattern
2/4 time

Step
Polka step—step, close, step

Position
Couples facing, both hands joined

The Dance
1. Place left heel to side. Place left toe behind right foot, left

heel raised. Take one polka step to the left, then one polka step to the right.

Repeat all.

2. Polka around room. Boy places hands at girl's waist, and girl places hands on boy's shoulders.

Figure 7–6. Heel-and-toe Polka

NELLIE GRAY

Rhythmic Pattern
2/4 time
Step
Square-dance step (see page 170)
Position
Square sets of eight

$$\begin{matrix} \text{G} & \text{B} \\ \text{B} & \quad\quad \text{G} \\ \text{G} & \quad\quad \text{B} \\ \text{B} & \text{G} \end{matrix}$$

The Dance

1. Join hands, circle left. Promenade back. First couple turn off to right.

   Four hands around. Swing opposite lady. Four hands around. Swing partner.

   Lead to next couple and repeat all.

   Lead to third couple and repeat all.

2. Face partners all. Dos-à-dos (partners pass right shoulders, taking three steps forward; without turning around, each takes one step to the right and moves back into place). Swing corner lady.

   Face corner lady. Dos-à-dos. Swing own partner.

Men to center with a left-hand star. Swing opposite lady. Ladies to center with a right-hand star. Swing own partner.

Repeat 2 on opposite side of set.

Promenade all.

Repeat all with all couples.

FIRST TWO LADIES

Rhythmic Pattern

  6/8 time, counted two beats to each measure

Step

  Square-dance step (see page 170)

Position

  Sets of eight in quadrille formation; the couples are numbered 1 to 8

The Dance

  1. "First two ladies over and by the opposite stand." Girls from couples 1 and 2 change places.

   "Second two ladies over and all join hands." Girls from couples 3 and 4 change places and all join hands.

   "Honor to your neighbor and honor your partners all." All bow to corners, then bow to partners.

   "Then you swing your partners and promenade the hall." All swing partners, then promenade.

  2. All promenade.

NIXIE POLKA

Parts of the Music

  A, four short phrases (measures 1 through 4); B, two phrases (measure 5 to 6, 7 to 8)

Rhythmic Pattern

  3/4 time

Steps

  Bleking step—with a jump, place left heel diagonally in front of the body and hold; repeat with the right

  Running step

Position

  Single circle all facing center. Leader stands in center with hands on hips.

The Dance

1. For part A of the music, all place hands on hips. Leader selects a child and dances facing him. On phrases 1 and 2, leader does bleking step left and right, then repeats on phrases 3 and 4.

2. On phrase 1 of part B, all children clap hands; the leader, with a little jump, turns around and starts running, followed by the dancer in front of whom he stood.

   On phrase 2, they continue running around the center of the circle, then stop in front of another dancer with two stamps on the last two notes of the phrase.

   The dance repeats until all children join the line in the center of the circle.

DONKEY DANCE

Parts of the Music

Eight phrases, two measures each

Rhythmic Pattern

2/4 time

Steps

Cross step—cross left foot in front of right, step left, then step right with right foot (let knees bend slightly as the step is taken); repeat with the right foot crossing first.

Jump step—jump once touching right heel in front; jump touching left heel in front; jump touching right heel in front and hold.

Position

Single circle with hands joined

The Dance

1. On phrases 1 and 2, move to the right in the circle with the cross step, the left foot crossing first; repeat this step four times. On the last step, touch the right toe to the side instead of stepping on it.

2. On phrases 3 and 4, repeat to the left, first crossing right foot in front of left.

3. On phrases 5 to 8, jump step four times.

POP GOES THE WEASEL

Parts of the Music

A, two phrases, repeated; B, two phrases, repeated

Rhythmic Pattern
6/8 time, counted two beats to each measure
Steps
Walking step, skipping step, sliding step
Position
Double line of three couples, partners facing (these sets of six may be spaced around the room in a large circle).
The Dance
1. On phrase 1, of part A of the music, the head couple separate, turn away from set, and walk down outside the set.

   On phrase 2, the head couple return to place.

   On phrase 1, the head couple slide down the center of the set, both hands joined.

   On phrase 2, the head couple slide back up the center, timing it so that they finish the phrase facing the second girl.

2. On phrases 1 and 2 of part B, the head couple join hands with the second girl, making a small circle of three; they skip around this small circle clockwise, timing their steps so that they have the second girl in the center of the set facing her partner for the word "Pop." This is the signal in the music for the head couple to make an arch with their joined hands and to "pop" the visiting girl out of the small circle of three back to place. They immediately reach over to the second boy and continue the small circle of three with him.

   This continues with the third girl, then the third boy. The first couple then remain at the foot of the set.

   The whole dance is repeated twice, so that each couple dances in the head couple's position.

Variations
To vary the dance, have more than three couples in the set. Each odd-numbered couple dance with the even-numbered couple below them in the second part of the dance. When an even-numbered couple reach the top of the set, they wait during one round of the dance and then dance with the next couple down the set.

To vary the dance without having more than three couples in a set, the partners—after doing the dance in the standard way described above—move toward each other, bow, and return to place on one phrase; then pass right shoulders and progress forward to meet a new couple on the next phrase. They repeat the dance with this new set.

MAYPOLE DANCE

Parts of the Music
A, two phrases, repeated; B, two phrases, repeated; C, two phrases, repeated
Rhythmic Pattern
6/8 time, counted two beats to each measure
Steps
Walking step, skipping step
Position
Double circle facing clockwise around the maypole, girls on boys' right. Ribbons are held in right hand about shoulder high.
The Dance
1. To part A of the music, take sixteen walking steps clockwise.

   To part B, take sixteen walking steps counterclockwise.

   To part C, face center in single circle, girls on boys' right. Take four skips forward toward pole, then four skips out to place. Repeat.
2. To part A, take eight skip-steps around partner to left, then eight skip-steps around partner to right.

   To part B, boys skip four steps to center and return. Then girls skip four steps to center and return. Repeat.

   To part C, face partner in a single circle. Boys take sixteen skip-steps clockwise on inside, while girls take sixteen skip-steps counterclockwise on outside.
3. To part A, turn and return to place.

   To part B, face partner in a single circle and wind maypole with a grand right and left.

STUNTS AND SELF-TESTING ACTIVITIES

Because children in this age group show an interest in their muscular power and development, they require a carefully planned program of self-testing activities and conditioning exercises. Not only the larger muscles of the body—trunk, arms, and legs—but also the smaller muscles—hands and feet—need to be developed. The teacher should recognize individual strengths and weaknesses and provide individual and group activities to meet these needs. The children should understand the purposes of the activities and be directed to careful and purposeful evaluation of their progress.

Children participating in these activities need careful guidance in developing correct techniques and safety habits. Time for practice and effort should be controlled. Children, in their zeal to practice, must not be allowed to overexercise in these activities. Teachers alert to this tendency will alternate quiet, easy stunts with the more strenuous ones.

Dividing the class into small units of six or eight provides children with the opportunity for greater participation and enables teachers to supervise the activities more effectively. Permitting children who show outstanding ability to serve as group leaders not only gives the teacher an opportunity to move from group to group but also enables pupils to develop qualities of leadership. Children may improve the quality of their performance by practicing, by observing the proper techniques exhibited by other children, and by viewing illustrations which emphasize correct form.

Many stunts used in earlier grades should be continued with this age group. As the quality of performance improves, the results will be more satisfying.

Exercises for Muscle Development

1. **Stunts for Development of Arm and Shoulder Muscles**
   a. Seal walk. Place hands on floor, fingers spread and pointing ahead; extend body in horizontal position with weight on hands and toes. Travel forward on hands, dragging toes.
   b. Worm walk. Place hands on floor. Walk forward on hands until body is fully extended. Hold hands still and walk up to hands with feet. Continue moving forward, alternately walking on hands and feet.
   c. Long reach. Stand with toes on a line. Place hands on floor

in front of feet. Walk forward on hands as far as possible without letting body touch the floor. Reach forward and make a mark on the floor. Measure the distance from the line to the mark.

d. Coffee grinder. Place right hand on floor, arm straight and body straight, so that weight is taken on feet and hand only. Walk around the pivot hand, keeping head well back and body straight.

e. Wheelbarrow. In couples, first child places his hands on the floor while the second child grasps his partner's legs above the knees and raises them. They walk in this position. Partners change places.

2. **Stunts for Development of Leg and Back Muscles**

a. Bend and reach back. Stand with feet apart. Bend forward and reach back between the legs. Make a mark on floor as far back as possible. Keep knees straight.

b. Heel click. Stand with weight on both feet. Jump up, clicking heels together before landing.

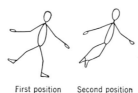

Figure 7–7. Heel Clicking

First position   Second position

c. Heel slap. Stand with hands behind back, thumbs locked. Jump, bending knees so that heels touch palms of hands.

Conditioning Exercises

The conditioning exercises included in this chapter help children respond quickly to direction and also, it is hoped, contribute to the development of muscular strength and flexibility. They are explained with counts, as children enjoy doing these exercises to music.

1. Stand with hands on hips, feet together.
    a. Jump, feet apart (count 1).
    b. Return to starting position (count 2).
    This may be done in time to music—2/4, 4/4, or 6/8 meter.

2. Stand with feet apart, arms extended sideward at shoulder height.
   a. Bending body forward, knees straight, touch right hand to left toe (count 1).
   b. Return to starting position (count 2).
   c. Touch left hand to right toe (count 3).
   d. Return to starting position (count 4).
   Using 3/4 meter, continue in units of four counts for twenty-eight or thirty-two counts.

3. Stand with arms at sides, feet together.
   a. Rise on toes, swinging arms forward (count 1).
   b. Bending knees, take squat position and touch fingers to floor between knees (count 2).
   c. Rise on toes, swinging arms forward (count 3).
   d. Return to starting position (count 4).

4. Stand with arms extended, hands clasped overhead, side-stride position.
   a. Bend truck to left (count 1).
   b. Continue bending trunk to the left, extending and pushing farther at each count (counts 2 and 3).
   c. Return to starting position (count 4).
   Exercise is repeated to the right. Continue using a 2/4 or 4/4 meter to a count of twenty-eight.

5. Stand with arms at sides, feet together.
   a. Take four short steps forward on toes (counts 1 to 4).
   b. Low squat position (count 5).
   c. Three hops in place in low squat position (counts 6 to 8).
   Using 2/4 meter, continue to twenty-eight or thirty-two counts in units of eight.

6. Stand in stride position with arms extended overhead.
   a. With knees straight, bend and twist body to the left; touch fingers to the floor (count 1).
   b. Return to starting position (count 2).
   c. Same as count one to the right (count 3).
   d. Return to starting position (count 4).
   Using 3/4 meter in groups of four counts, continue for sixteen or twenty counts.

7. Stand with arms at sides, feet together.
   a. Squat position, back straight, raise arms forward shoulder high (count 1).
   b. Return to starting position (count 2).
   c. With knees straight, bend trunk forward and touch fingers to toes (count 3).
   d. Return to starting position (count 4).

   Using 3/4 meter, continue slowly in units of four counts for twenty-eight to thirty-two counts.

8. Stand with arms at sides, feet together.
   a. Jog in place (counts 1 to 10).
   b. Knees high, run in place (counts 11 to 20).

   Using 2/4 meter, continue in units of twenty for sixty to eighty counts.

9. Stand with arms at sides, feet together.
   a. Raise left leg forward, with knees straight; swing arms forward at shoulder height (count 1).
   b. Balancing on one foot, move arms sideward (count 2).
   c. Move arms forward (count 3).
   d. Return to starting position (count 4). Repeat, raising left leg.

   Using 2/4 or 4/4 meter, continue in groups of four counts for a count of twenty-eight to thirty-two counts.

Track and Field Activities

Nine- and ten-year-old children show a definite interest in activities which test their skill and endurance as a group as well as individually. Simple track and field events help satisfy this interest. Emphasis should be placed on accuracy, skill, techniques, and fair play—on skillful performance rather than on winning. Track and field events—together with the competitive-games program, which constitutes a major part of the physical education program for this age group—offer a splendid opportunity for developing sound and satisfactory attitudes toward a sports program. The winner who has demonstrated skill, accuracy, and adherence to the rules should receive the admiration and respect of his fellow members. The loser who has demonstrated effort and fair play should also receive respect and admiration from his comrades. Both winner and loser should evaluate their performances in terms of effort, training, and participation. Track and field events should not be overemphasized, however, as a balanced program of activities should be maintained.

The following simple events are examples of the type suitable for this age group.

Running Broad Jump. This activity should be practiced only on playgrounds where it is possible to keep a soft, well-stirred pit. Use a smooth board 3 feet long, 6 inches wide, and 2 inches thick. It should be even with the ground at a distance of 3 feet from one end of the pit.

A jump is legal if the jumper strikes the ground with his take-off foot behind the edge of the take-off board nearest the pit. The distance of the jump is measured from the take-off board to the first break made in the earth by any part of the jumper's body.

Rules:

1. Each contestant has two tries, and his better performance is recorded.

2. A player receives no credit for a jump improperly taken, that is, running over the take-off board or extending toe over the edge of take-off board.

Shuttle Relay. Two lines are drawn 30 yards apart. Ten children comprise a team. Several teams compete against one another. Each team is divided into two groups. The first group count off 1, 3, 5, 7, 9, and the second group 2, 4, 6, 8, 10.

The first group stand behind the starting line in single file in numerical order. The second group stand in similar formation behind the other line, facing their teammates.

At a signal, number 1 from each team runs with the baton in his hand to his teammate number 2. Number 2 takes the baton, runs forward to his teammate number 3, and passes him the baton. This procedure continues until number 10 crosses the starting line. The team whose number 10 player crosses the starting line first wins.

Rules:

1. No player leaves the starting line until his teammate passes him the baton.

2. As each player completes his run, he sits down behind a retiring line, which is drawn 5 yards behind the starting line.

RL	SL		SL	RL
First group			Second group	
9, 7, 5, 3, 1	← 30 yards →		2, 4, 6, 8, 10	
9, 7, 5, 3, 1			2, 4, 6, 8, 10	
← 5 yards →			← 5 yards →	

SUMMARY

The period of growing up is a difficult one for both the children experiencing it and the adults who guide them during this time. It is important to think of these children, not in terms of a certain age level, but in terms of a maturity level. During this period, children progress at very different rates. Therefore, a program for them should be planned very skillfully. It should provide games and activities which satisfy the children's increasing desire for competition. It should develop skills that satisfy their growing aim for perfection. It should refine all previously learned skills while broadening the scope with new learnings.

This chapter explains the methods and materials that comprise such a program. It suggests procedures that help to bridge the gap evident in this growing-up period and to prepare children for the age of individuality discussed in Chapter 8.

QUESTIONS AND TOPICS FOR DISCUSSION

1. Discuss the term *maturity level*. How does it differ from *age level*?

2. Enumerate some of the problems that arise from the range in the maturity levels among nine- and ten-year-old children.

3. Why are team games especially satisfying to children of this age?

4. How does the extension of rhythmic experiences contribute to the growth of these children?

SUGGESTED ACTIVITY UNIT

Plan a unit in which physical education activities supplement a study of Mexican village life. The core of the unit might be a study of the basic needs of Mexican children, for the purpose of comparing and contrasting the ways in which the respective needs of Mexican and American children are met. There are innumerable rhythmic activities to enrich this study.

8. Program for the
Eleven- and
Twelve-year-olds

Individuality is the keynote of this age group. These children seem more individualistic in nature and development than do children of other age groups. A teacher of these children may well exclaim, "They have no notion of how children ought to grow!" Since the physical, mental, and emotional growth of the average child has been gradual during earlier years, it is disconcerting to observe the apparently erratic rate of growth and development during this period. Some of these children seem to "shoot up tall like an India-rubber ball" practically overnight. Some just as suddenly become much interested in the opposite sex. With these children, as with the nine- and ten-year-olds, the teacher must realize that maturity levels rather than age or grade levels should be the guides for determining suitable activities for them.

It is the responsibility of the teacher to be thoroughly acquainted with the characteristics of many age groups and to recognize and give thoughtful consideration to rates of physical growth and to levels of maturity. Teachers who are ever-conscious of these two factors recognize each new level of maturity as one containing the residue or background upon which new growth characteristics depend. Children of this age group, if adequately prepared and wisely guided, take with them into the adolescent period satisfactory behavior patterns, wholesome attitudes, and rich understandings of comparative values, thus avoiding a period of difficult adjustments.

Growth and Development. This is a period of transition. For those children who experience the "preadolescent spurt," there is a period of rapid skeletal and muscular growth. If skeletal growth and muscular development are out of proportion, poor control will follow. Rapid and uneven growth causes awkward-

186

ness, restlessness, and apparent laziness. These children grow fastest the year before the puberty cycle is completed. First there is a rapid growth in height, then in weight. The development of the heart, however, continues to lag behind this rapid growth, and other parts of the body may also show uneven growth. Girls often reach maturity as much as two years earlier than boys.

Children who are not approaching puberty remain much like the nine- or ten-year-olds in physical appearance and development. As stated before, maturity is an individual matter, and in every classroom of children from ten to twelve or thirteen years old a teacher finds some children who have already matured, some who are about to mature, and some who are still young boys and girls physically, socially, and emotionally.

These children like to improve their abilities and master skills. They are now able to maintain a long period of intellectual concentration. Although they are able to do effective abstract thinking, they still prefer problems arising from concrete situations. They are usually interested in scientific experiments. There is a noticeable increase in self-direction and a more serious attitude toward work. They set their own goals and, if given the opportunity to do so, carry out many individual responsibilities.

Physical growth has a direct bearing on achievement in general. The child who grows too fast may become a school problem unless wisely and understandingly guided.

Because there is such a wide range in physical maturity within the group, there are consequently many temperamental differences. Children who grow too fast become shy and self-conscious; little ones worry because they have not grown. All seem to have changing moods and interests. Children approaching adolescence often become overcritical, rebellious, and uncooperative. Many of them think they "know it all." They go to extremes. They return to habits they had when very young. They bite their nails and daydream. They are oversensitive.

There is often a teasing, antagonistic attitude between boys and girls. A teacher with a sense of humor can easily change a teasing, antagonistic attitude into a teasing, friendly attitude. These children like adults with a sense of humor. They like to know that older people have a warm feeling toward them. An adult who nags or talks down to them seldom enjoys working with them.

Their Needs. These children need a sense of belonging, a feeling of acceptance, first by the group and then by the adult. A teacher who recognizes that their need for group approval is stronger than their need for adult approval builds up within the group the importance of each individual. These children need kindly guidance and opportunities to make decisions. They need counseling to learn how to cope with the difficult feelings they are experiencing. They need guidance to appreciate the importance and the essentiality of giving in to others now and then.

Planning a Program. To meet the needs of such a group, a school program must be skillfully planned, carefully organized, and enthusiastically executed.

Thoughtful planning of physical education activities that are well-integrated with other phases of the school program may have a marked effect on the dispositions of the class as a whole and of individuals within the class. Although there are interest differences between boys and girls at this age, as well as between the more and less mature members of the same sex, there are physical education activities that appeal to all. A program which provides opportunities to practice self-testing activities and creative rhythmic ideas satisfies the children's need to act as individuals rather than as a group.

A stimulating program of challenging team games, rhythmic activities, and interesting dances often unites a heterogeneous group of individuals into a group that is class-conscious and eager to have fun as a class.

Previous chapters describe activities motivated by the teacher or by children in the class. This chapter explains the influence that a supervisor of physical education had on one group of children ranging in age from nine to thirteen. Although these children varied in height and weight and in level of maturity, they had developed an exceptionally fine spirit of oneness. They were proud of themselves as a group. They appreciated one another's abilities and tolerated individual weaknesses. They liked to play and dance together, and the physical education period was the hub around which the wheel of their day turned. A visit by the supervisor of physical education was an exciting time because they were confident of her appreciation and eager to receive her suggestions for something new.

One day they had a wonderful time showing her how many dances they had learned. When they went back to their places and sat looking expectantly at her, she said, "Wasn't that fun!" They liked her because she never spoiled their fun by criticizing minor imperfections in their performance. She recognized their own feelings about an activity. They knew that she was ready to help them when they and their children experienced difficulties, but that she was just as ready to enjoy with them their *pleasure* in what they considered a "job well done." Of course, to them, no part of physical education was a job; it was all fun. But some adults could take away this fun and make it a job just by the expression on their faces. These children knew by the expression on their supervisor's face that she liked their dancing, and they were happy.

She continued, "You put so much spirit into your dancing! I'd like to have you dance at a celebration in the city auditorium. Would you be willing to do that?" That was another thing that endeared the supervisor to these children. She made them feel important. She made them feel that they were doing her a favor when she gave them an opportunity to perform for others.

Their enthusiastic responses assured her that they would prepare themselves for the I Am an American Day celebration. She suggested that they create their own dance patterns for the "Victory Polka," a popular tune at that time. She played it on the piano and told them that she would record it for them. After a few minutes of discussion, they decided that they would represent the Polish-American people. They were given the entire responsibility for planning the dance and of designing and making their own costumes.

Thus a unit of interesting activities was motivated by a supervisor who realized how important a stimulating challenge could be to such a group. These children worked hard to prove that they were worthy of the confidence placed in them. They practiced combinations of schottische steps, two-steps, and heel-and-toe polka steps and danced them to different phrases of the "Victory Polka." They finally worked out an effective set of patterns and called for their supervisor's approval and suggestions. She was generous with both. She suggested that they teach their dance to the other sixth-grade class in the building and invite these children to dance with them at the celebration. They welcomed this suggestion; thus the children and teachers of these two classes enjoyed working together.

For three weeks, learning the dance was the activity of primary interest and importance to these two groups. However, it was not their only interest and activity. They had to design and make their costumes, and they needed to learn more about Poland and the Polish people.

At the end of three weeks they had perfected their dance to their own satisfaction and that of their teachers and supervisor. In addition, they had made their costumes. They had painted stripes on unbleached cotton, from which they made the girls' skirts and the boys' brightly colored sashes. They completed their costumes with white blouses for all and bright headbands for the girls. They had compiled their information into booklets which later became a part of a *Book of Nations and Their Peoples*. The culmination was, of course, the program for I Am an American Day. However, the true value of the unit was in the day-by-day experience of working together and in the spirit that would prompt the children and their teachers to summarize their activity by echoing the words of their supervisor, which were, "Wasn't that fun!"

Every part of physical education can be as effective as the preceding unit in challenging the individuals of a class and in forming a class into a cooperative working unit.

Track and field events give children an opportunity to compete as individuals and as teams. Team games, so popular with children of this age, not only develop skill in the game but also instill an appreciation of the importance of rules and a sense of fair play. Self-testing activities provide children with an opportunity to know themselves, their capabilities, and their power of endurance. Through these self-testing activities young people measure their own progress, comparing each performance with a previous one.

the circle when kicking; or (c) kicks a foul ball, unless he already has two strikes.

Outs: An out is made if (a) kicker makes three strikes; (b) a placed ball is kicked foul by kicker (after four balls, kicker places ball in circle and place-kicks it); (c) Indian club at home is knocked down by kicker or bowler; (d) fair ball knocks down field club before striking ground; (e) fielder catches a fly, fair or foul; (f) runner is hit by fair, kicked ball; (g) runner knocks down any Indian club; (h) club ahead of runner is knocked down by the baseman; (i) runner fails to round all the bases in order; (j) runner interferes with player or ball; (k) runner runs inside the diamond in front of any club.

Indoor—Large-group Games

A. Indoor Volleyball
1. *Purpose*

   To increase skill in volleying and serving a ball
2. *Equipment*

   Regulation volleyball, net, and playing area. If no gymnasium or playroom is available, the classroom may be used and a string may serve as net.
3. *Description*

   Divide the class into two teams of equal number. The formation is the same as that described for outdoor volleyball in Chapter 7, page 154. The same rules are observed. Players should be encouraged to develop these habits of play:

   a. In volleying, use both hands when it will be advantageous to do so.

   b. Look for the unguarded area of opponent's court and guide the ball to this spot.

   c. Play as a team, not as individuals; pass from one to another.

   d. Keep your eyes on the ball at all times.

B. Aerial Bombardment
1. *Purpose*

   To improve aim in throwing a ball and to increase skill in dodging and catching a ball

2. *Equipment*
An indoor volleyball or partially deflated volleyball

3. *Description* (see Figure 8–1)
The playing area is divided in the middle by a line. The end zones are marked off as on the diagram. Each team has one-half the playing area of the court. The ball is tossed between two players to determine which team throws the ball first. The captain of the team that wins first play may throw the ball or pass it to a teammate who throws it at a player on the opposing team. The object is to hit an opponent with the ball before it touches the floor. If a player is so hit, he goes to the end court behind the opposing team.

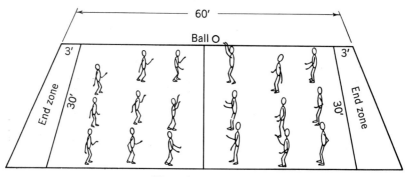

Figure 8–1. Aerial Bombardment

He may return to the game if he recovers the ball when it rolls near him. To recover the ball, he may step with one foot out of the end zone. A player may attempt to catch the ball when it is thrown at him. If he succeeds in catching it, the player who threw it must go to the end zone. The winning team is the one with the fewest players in the end zone at the end of the play period.

Outdoor—Small-group Games

A. Figure 8 Relay

1. *Purpose*
To increase control and speed in running

2. *Equipment*
Three Indian clubs or cans for each team

3. *Description* (see Figure 8–2)
Players are arranged in lines back of the starting line, as shown in the diagram. At the signal from the leader, the first runner runs up and, passing to the right of the first club, starts weaving between the clubs and returns (see diagram). When the first runner finishes, he tags the next player, and so on until all have run. The first team back into the original lineup wins.

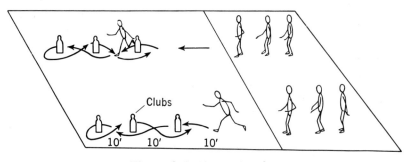

Figure 8–2. Figure 8 Relay

B. Chinese Relay

1. *Purpose*
To increase power of concentration

2. *Equipment*
None

3. *Description*
Players line up in single file behind the leader, an equal number of players in each row. A goal line is drawn 25 feet from the starting line. The second and third players step up on either side of the leader, their backs toward the starting line, and the three link arms. At a signal from the leader, they travel to the goal line and without turning around return to the starting line. The leader unhooks, going to the end of the line, while the next player in line hooks on. The first team with all players back in the original position wins.

C. Team Broad Jump

1. *Purpose*

   To develop ability to jump

2. *Equipment*

   A stick or piece of chalk for marking heelprints

3. *Description*

   Leaders of each team line up behind the starting line. The leader in each team broad-jumps as far as possible. The second player on each team marks the heelprints, or the handprints if the player falls backward, then stands with his toes just behind that line. From this point the second player jumps, and so on until each has had a turn. The team jumping the farthest from the starting line wins.

D. Tunnel Relay

1. *Purpose*

   To increase accuracy in aiming and rolling a ball

2. *Equipment*

   8-inch rubber ball or soccer ball for each team

3. *Description*

   The teams line up with the leaders standing on the starting line. Each leader holds a ball until the signal is given to begin. The ball is then rolled down the line between the legs of the players. If the ball goes out of the line, the player in front of whom the ball passed recovers the ball and restarts it from his position in line. When the last player in the line gets the ball, he runs forward to the starting line and starts the ball in play, as at the beginning of the game. The winning team is the one which first succeeds in getting all players back into starting position.

E. Over-and-under Relay

1. *Purpose*

   a. To develop accuracy in passing

   b. To increase the power of concentration

2. *Equipment*

   8-inch rubber ball or soccer ball for each team

3. *Description*

   The first player on each team stands on the starting line,

holding the ball. At a signal, the first player passes the ball overhead to the second player. The second player passes the ball between his legs to the third player, who passes the ball overhead. Play continues by alternating over and under until the last player receives the ball. The last player goes to the starting line and repeats the overhead pass. If the ball is dropped or rolled out of the line, it must be recovered and started where it left the line. The winning team is the one which first succeeds in getting back to its original starting position.

Indoor—Small-group Games

A. Basketball Relay

1. *Purpose*
   a. To develop skill in the chest pass
   b. To increase speed and accuracy in throwing and catching
2. *Equipment*
   A basketball or soccer ball for each team
3. *Description*
   Groups of ten comprise the teams. The leader of each team stands facing his teammates. Each leader has a basketball. At a signal, the leader throws the ball to the first player on his team, using the chest pass. The first player returns the ball, using the same pass, and runs to the end of the line. The leader then passes the ball to the next player, who returns it in the same way, and so on until each player has had a turn. If a player drops the ball, he must recover it and return to his place in line before he passes the ball to the leader. The winning team is the one which first completes the passing.

B. Push-the-ball Relay

1. *Purpose*
   To increase muscular coordination and control
2. *Equipment*
   An 8-inch rubber ball and a wand (a sawed-off broom handle may be used) for the leader of each line

3. *Description*

On a signal, the first player in each line pushes the ball to the goal line 30 feet away and returns to the next player. The next player repeats the process, and so on until each player has had a turn. The winning team is the one that first succeeds in getting back to starting positions.

C. **Forward-pass Relay**

This relay is naturally more popular with boys than with girls.

1. *Purpose*

To develop accuracy and speed in passing and catching a football

2. *Equipment*

A football for each team

3. *Description* (see Figure 8–3)

The members of the team are numbered and lined up, as shown in diagram. Number 1 players have the football. At

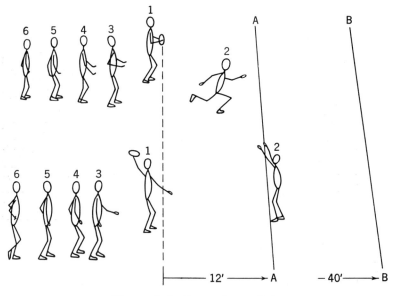

Figure 8–3. Forward-pass Relay

a given signal, number 2 player on each team runs to the line which is 12 feet from the starting line. At the line, he turns to catch the football, which number 1 throws to him. Number 1 goes to the end of the line after throwing the ball. When number 2 catches or recovers the ball, he runs back and touches the hand of number 3, who runs to line A. Number 2 player stands to the left of his team and passes the ball to number 3, who has to run to line A. This sequence continues until each player has both passed and caught the ball. Number 1, who was first to throw the ball, is touched by number 9, who then throws the ball to him. When number 1 receives the ball at line A, he runs 40 feet to line B. The winning team is the one whose number 1 player first crosses line B.

RHYTHMS AND DANCE

Although eleven- and twelve-year-olds have already acquired a background of rhythmic experience, they need many opportunities to practice the fundamental rhythmic movements and to extend their experience with the more advanced patterns of response. There should be no lapse in their education or in their opportunities to enjoy the activities made possible by their increased skill. Poise, enjoyment in rhythmic expression, and an eagerness to participate in social activities are the result of an adequately planned program.

Young people in this age group continue to need encouragement to respond freely and creatively. Any originality displayed should receive recognition and respect. By extending the activities in the natural rhythmic patterns of locomotion to include variations and combinations of these rhythms, children gain confidence in themselves. They improve their ability to recognize and to respond to many musical meters.

Ball bouncing, rope twirling, and rope jumping to music help the self-conscious child forget himself as he concentrates on the ball or the rope. He has the pleasure of responding to music and achieving a skill simultaneously. If encouraged to create a variety of activities with ropes and balls, these children are ready to create their own dance patterns. A teacher who merely suggests a pattern may expect a generous response.

The program of dancing, however, should be carefully planned, guided, and directed. These children need the experience of learning and enjoying many kinds of dances. A dance program should include folk dancing, circle dancing, square dancing, and some simple social dancing. Through a continuity and extension of guidance and experience in every aspect of rhythm and dance, these eleven- and twelve-year-olds gracefully bridge the gap that often presents difficulty at this age.

Children enjoy reviewing and re-creating responses to rhythmic activities of former years. They enjoy reviewing dances previously learned and experiencing the challenge of new dances. Several dances are described and explained on the following pages. Music for these dances will be found in the Appendix. Suggested recordings are listed at the end of Part Two, pages 218 and 219.

VIRGINIA REEL

The Virginia Reel is one of the most popular folk dances of the United States. Different versions of the dance are found in different sections of the country, but in one form or another it is usually a favorite wherever it is known.

Some people do the first part of the dance with the head lady and foot gentleman executing the figure, followed by the head gentleman and foot lady. In order that everyone may have the fun of dancing and not have to wait for this part, teachers may follow the directions given below for partners to dance the first part with each other.

Rhythmic Pattern
  4/4 time
Steps
  Square-dance step—a dragging run, with an occasional catch step if the dancer wishes (feet kept close to the floor, knees bent to avoid bouncing)
  Slide step
Position
  Two lines of eight couples, facing each other and about eight short steps apart

The Dance

1. Forward three square-dance steps toward partner and bow. Return.

   Move forward to partner, join right hands, and circle around. Return.

   Move forward to partner, join left hands, and circle around. Return.

   Move forward to partner, join both hands, and circle around. Return.

   Move forward to partner, dos-à-dos (back to back) passing right shoulders. Return.

   Move forward to partner, dos-à-dos passing left shoulders. Return.

2. The head couple slide down the center of the set and return to their original positions, then start the reel.

   The Reel: The head couple join right hands and swing once and a half around, so that the girl finishes facing the boys' line and the boy finishes facing the girls' line.

   The head girl takes the next boy's left hand and turns him once in place; at the same time the head boy is turning the second girl in place with left hands joined.

   The head couple then meet in the center of the set, join right hands, and circle once around until they are facing the next person in line.

   The head girl joins left hands with the third boy and circles him; at the same time, the head boy joins left hands with the third girl and circles her.

   The head couple again join right hands and circle in the center of the set.

   The reel continues in this manner until they reach the foot of the set. The head couple then slide up the center of the set to their original positions.

3. Cast Off: All couples turn so that they face head couple. The head girl leads the line of girls to the foot of the set by turning to the outside; the head boy does the same. When

the head couple meet at the foot of the set, they join hands and make an arch for the others to pass under. When all are under the arch, partners face each other; all step away from their partner, and the dance is repeated with the second couple as the new head couple.

The whole dance is repeated seven times, until all have been in the head couple's position.

PORTLAND FANCY

Rhythmic Pattern

6/8 time, counted two beats to each measure

Steps

Walking step, square-dance step (see page 202)

Position

Sets of eight, two couples in a line of four facing an opposite line of four; sets of eight arranged around the room as spokes of wheels

The Dance

1. Circle Left: All join hands in sets of eight and take either a walking or a square-dance step to the left, for all of part A of the music, sixteen steps in all.

2. Down Center and Back: Couple nearest the center of the room join both hands, slide four steps to the foot of the set, and return. Foot couple repeat to the head of the set and return.

3. Grand Right and Left: Partners face each other with right hands joined. Each dancer walks around the set, giving his left hand to the next person, his right hand to the next, and so on, alternating in this way until he is back in place.

4. Ladies' Change: Girls diagonally across from each other pass to opposite side, touching right hands as they pass. They give left hand to opposite boy, who turns them once and sends them back home. Repeat, girls passing, touching right hands and giving left hand to partner, who turns them into their place.

5. Forward and Back: Lines of four join hands, walk forward three steps, bow and curtsy, and return to place. Then they walk forward, drop hands, pass right shoulders with the

person directly opposite, and advance to meet a new set of four.

Dance is repeated with new set of four.

RED RIVER VALLEY

And you lead right on down the valley,
And you circle to the left and to the right,
And you swing with the girl in the valley,
And you swing with your Red River girl.

Parts of the Music
One part, four phrases
Rhythmic Pattern
4/4 time
Steps
Walking step, square-dance step (see page 202)
Position
Large circle of couples. Every other couple faces the couple behind so that there are small sets of four children around the circle.
The Dance
"And you lead right on down the valley." Couples walk past couple they now face, passing to the right. Meeting the next couple, they join hands in a circle of four.

"And you circle to the left and to the right." They circle four steps left, turn, circle back to the right, and finish facing opposite couple.

"And you swing with the girl in the valley." Boys cross over and take opposite girl in social-dance position and turn her.

"And you swing with your Red River girl." Boys go back and swing own girl once; they finish facing as at the beginning of the dance.

Entire dance is repeated; couples move out to meet a new couple each time.

SICILIAN CIRCLE

This American dance is an excellent mixer since each time the dance is repeated, it is done with a different couple. During an evening of square dancing, it is often used as a round dance between quadrilles.

Parts of the Music

A, two phrases; B, two phrases; C, two phrases

Rhythmic Pattern

6/8 time, counted two beats to each measure

Steps

Square-dance step (see page 202)

Buzz step—one foot kept on the same spot while the other advances, turning the individual

Position

Double circle around the room, boys with their partners on their right and every other couple reversed to face the couple behind them. The circle is composed of these small sets of four children.

The Dance

1. On phrase 1 of part A of the music, four hands around: Each set of four join hands in a small circle and take the square-dance step around the circle clockwise.

   On phrase 2, repeat going counterclockwise.

2. On phrase 1 of part B, right and left: Both couples cross over, the ladies passing between the men and giving the men their right hands as they pass. Partners now take left hands and exchange places on the opposite side of the square from where they started. They give right hands to the opposite lady and pass back across; then give left hands to their own partner and come back to home position.

   On phrase 2, buzz partner: For a square-dance turn, partners stand with right sides together; the boy puts his right arm around the girl's waist; either the girl holds onto the boy's left shoulder or he takes her right hand in his left and she holds her skirt with her left hand. In this position, partners turn with eight buzz steps.

3. On phrase 1 of part C, ladies chain: Girls cross, giving right hands as they pass each other and left hands to opposite boy; boy places his right hand around girl's waist in back, turns her around in front of him, and faces her home.

On phrase 2, girls return home, giving right hands to each other as they pass and left hands to their own partner; partner places his right arm around girl's waist and turns her into her place on his right side.

NORWEGIAN MOUNTAIN DANCE

Parts of the Music

A, two phrases, repeated; B, two phrases, repeated

Rhythmic Pattern

3/4 time, counted one beat to each quarter note, with the first note of each measure heavily accented

Steps

Running steps are used throughout this dance. The first step of each measure is accented by stamping on that count and bending the whole body in the same direction. This gives the effect of mountain climbing.

Position

In groups of threes, representing two mountain climbers and their guide. Number 1 is the guide; number 2, a climber, is to the left and in back of the guide; and number 3, the other climber, is to the right and in back of guide. Number 1 extends his arms in back and takes the hands of the couple in back. Throughout the first part of the dance, 1 appears to be pulling 2 and 3 behind him. These groups of dancers are spaced around the room in a large circle formation.

The Dance

1. Beginning with the right foot, all run forward, accenting the first count of each measure and bending the body to the accented side. This is continued throughout part A of the music.

2. For part B of the music, 1 runs backward three steps under the arch made by 2 and 3, who take the three running steps in place (measure 1).

   After passing under the arch, 1 continues with three more steps in place; 2 and 3 take their three running steps in place (measure 2).

   With six running steps, 2 passes in front of 1 and turns inward once around in place under 1's right arm (measures 3 and 4).

With six short running steps, 3 turns inward once around in place under 1's right arm (measures 5 and 6).

With six short running steps, 1 turns under his own right arm. This brings the three back to their original positions (measures 7 and 8).

Throughout part 2, the dancers continue to hold hands, and each dancer takes his running steps in place when it is not his turn to change position.

Figure 8–4. Norwegian Mountain March

KANAFASKA

The *kanafaska* is the peasant woman's full skirt, which is made of striped cotton material.

Parts of the Music

A, four phrases of two measures each; B, four phrases of two measures each, repeated

Rhythmic Pattern

2/4 time

Steps

Polka—three very short running steps and a hop on the fourth step

Gallop—running step, close, step, close; same foot always in the lead

Position

Quadrille formation, all facing center of set

The Dance

1. On phrase 1 of part A of the music, couples 1 and 3 exchange places with four gallop steps, passing to the right.

    On phrase 2, couples 2 and 4 exchange places with four gallop steps, passing to the right.

    On phrase 3, couples 1 and 3 return to place with four gallop steps.

    On phrase 4, couples 2 and 4 do the same.

2. For part B of the music, all couples take waist-shoulder position (boy with hands on girl's waist, girl with hands on partner's shoulders, leaning away from partner). They polka counterclockwise around the circle back to original places, taking eight polka steps.

    First girl visits around: She claps hands on first count and polkas to the second boy, who takes her in waist-shoulder position and dances the polka once around inside the set. Second boy finishes beside his partner. This is repeated with third boy and with the fourth boy.

    All couples take waist-shoulder position and dance the polka once around to place.

    Second girl visits around.

    All couples polka once around the set.

    Third girl visits around.

    All couples polka around the set.

    Fourth girl visits around.

    All couples polka once around the set.

    On the last count of the music, when dancing the polka in couples, the boys may "jump" the girls high in the air. At the same time the girls give a shriek.

CAPTAIN JINKS

Verse

> When Captain Jinks comes home at night,
> You pass your partner on the right.
> You swing your neighbor so polite,
> For that's the style in the army.

Chorus

> All join hands and circle right,
> Circle right, circle right,
> All join hands and circle right,
> For that's the style in the army.

Parts of the Music

Verse, four phrases; chorus, four phrases

Rhythmic Pattern

6/8 time, counted two beats to each measure

Steps

Step-close-step—step forward on right, close left to right; step back left, close right to left

Walking step

Position

Single circle, partners standing side by side and facing center

The Dance

1. "When Captain Jinks comes home at night." Step-close-step to center, starting right with a stamp on the first step. Repeat going back, starting with left.

   "You pass your partner on the right." Join right hands with partner, pass partner, and meet the next partner.

   "You swing your neighbor so polite, for that's the style in the army." In social-dance position, turn new partner.

2. As the chorus is sung, boys place their partners on their right, and all join hands in circle and walk around the circle to the right.

Repeat dance with a new partner each time.

TEXAS SCHOTTISCHE

Rhythmic Pattern

4/4 time

Position

Couples in a double circle, partners side by side, all facing counterclockwise with hands joined in skating position

The Dance

1. Starting with the right foot, take two schottische steps forward—step, close, step-hop (two measures).

Take four step-hops forward—right, left, right, left (two measures).

Repeat all (four measures).

2. Face partner, hands on hips. Starting with the right foot, take one schottische step sideward, then repeat to the left (two measures).

Join right hands with partner. Starting with the right foot, take four step-hops around partner (two measures).

Repeat all (four measures).

3. Same as 1 (eight measures).

4. Starting with the right foot, place heel, then toe in front of other foot; then take three running steps forward (two measures).

Repeat with left foot (two measures).

Face partner and join both hands. Starting with the right foot, take four step-hops around partner (two measures).

Boy stands in place, girl takes four step-hops forward to meet the next boy as a new partner (two measures).

STUNTS AND SELF-TESTING ACTIVITIES

Systematic practice in stunts and self-testing activities develops satisfying experiences in body coordination. Children of this age are interested in increasing body strength and skill.

Running and jumping activities increase the individual's power of endurance. Trunk bending and twisting and rolling, chinning, and push-up activities develop the muscles of arms, legs, shoulders, and abdomen. Stunts and activities suggested for the younger children should be continued and improved. When the familiar ones have been remastered, a more difficult group may be taught.

Exercises for Muscle Development

1. **Squat Thrust**
   a. Place hands on floor between knees.
   b. With a jump, extend the legs backward, with weight on hands and toes. Body should be in a straight line.

     c. With a jump, return to squat position.

     d. Stand erect.

  This should be done eight or ten times in succession.

2. **Push-ups**

     a. Lie on floor.

     b. With hands at shoulder level, push up until weight is on hands and toes. Body should be in a straight line.

     c. Lower body until chest touches the floor.

  This pushing up and lowering the body should be continued, without pausing for rest, as many times as possible.

3. **Bear Dance or Cossack Step**

     a. Squat position.

     b. Place hands on hips or raise arms sideward.

     c. With a jump, extend one leg out in front.

     d. Rapidly extend one leg and then the other. The skill of keeping one's balance while alternating the extension of legs is difficult to acquire.

4. **Knee Walk**

     a. Kneel and grasp ankles.

     b. Walk forward, keeping head erect and weight forward.

Figure 8–5. Cossack Step

Figure 8–6. Knee Walk

5. **Foot Throw**

     a. Place a soccer ball between the feet.

     b. Jump, tossing the ball into the air.

  With correct timing, the individual should be able to catch the ball.

6. **Grapevine**

     a. Stand pigeon-toed.

     b. Pivot on right heel and left toe.

    c. Bring heels together, toes apart.

    d. Pivot on left heel and right toe.

    e. Bring toes together again.

    f. Continue four steps to the right and then four steps to the left.

7. Horizontal Balance

    a. Stand on right foot.

    b. Raise the arms shoulder high and extend left leg backward; bend trunk forward until body and left leg are at right angles to the supporting leg.

    c. Return to position.

    d. Raise arms shoulder high and extend right leg backward; bend forward until body and right leg are at right angles with left leg.

    e. Continue this exercise, alternating left and right.

Conditioning

Because this is the age of irregularities in growth as well as in behavior patterns, a careful program of conditioning exercises should be planned. These children need exercises, but they must be guarded against overpracticing any of them.

Exercises should be chosen to meet any special needs that are evident in the group or in individuals.

A. Exercises to Increase Flexibility

  1. Stand with feet pointing straight ahead, and slightly apart.

    a. Bend the upper trunk forward.

    b. Relax fingers and arms, let head hang freely.

    c. Bend knees slightly.

    d. Bounce several times and return to a good standing position.

  2. The same exercise may be done with the knees remaining straight and a definite count for trunk bending and arm lowering, as follows.

    a. Position (count 1)

    b. Trunk forward bend, and arms lower, with an attempt to touch floor (count 2)

    c. Trunk raise, and arms upward stretch (count 3)

    d. Position (count 4)

This can be done to musical accompaniment, using 4/4 meter.

B. Exercises to Increase Endurance

1. Stand at attention
   a. Run in place with a normal lifting of feet for ten counts.
   b. Run in place, lifting knees high in front, for ten to twenty counts.

   Continue in rhythm for at least eighty counts. This may be done to musical accompaniment, using 2/4 meter.

2. Stand at attention
   a. To side-stride position, jump, clapping hands over head.
   b. To starting position, return.

   This may be done to musical accompaniment, using 2/4 or 6/8 meter.

C. Exercises to Improve Balance

These exercises are explained with counts, as they are more easily adapted to musical accompaniment if counts are given.

1. Stand with left foot 6 or 8 inches in front of right, hands clasped on top of head.
   a. To squat position, drop, and sit on right heel (count 1).
   b. From this position, spring up and change position of feet while in air (count 2).
   c. To squat position, drop, and sit on left heel.
   d. From this position, spring up and change positions again.

   This exercise is counted in *un*even rhythm (1–2, 1–2, 1–2) for at least sixteen counts. It may be done to musical accompaniment, using 6/8 meter.

2. Stand at attention
   a. To forward-stride position, jump, left foot about 18 inches in front of right. Swing right arm forward and left arm backward.
   b. Reverse positions of arms and legs, right foot in front, left arm forward and right arm backward.

   This exercise may continue in rhythm for at least sixteen counts. It may be done to musical accompaniment, using 2/4 or 4/4 meter.

Track and Field Events

Eleven- and twelve-year-old children show an increased interest in track and field events. Having participated in simple relay racing and jumping, they are ready for events which require more endurance, coordination, and skill.

Track and field events are of value only if they are used to help children develop in accordance with their individual potentialities. Used correctly, they are self-testing activities in which each participant competes against his own record. In team activities, competition should be among children of similar age and ability level.

In a well-planned track and field program, emphasis is placed on improvement in the skills of running, jumping, and throwing and on the development of favorable attitudes toward competitive activities.

As endurance, speed, agility, and strength increase, each individual learns to respect the ability of his opponents and develops habits of good sportsmanship in individual and group competition.

Standards of achievement may be set by each group after individual records have been compiled. If each participant shows improvement in his own record, participates successfully to add to the team score, practices safety rules, and forms the habit of "sticking" to what he starts, a class or school program of track and field events is successful.

The following track and field activities are suitable for eleven- and twelve-year-old children.

1. **Activities That Develop Proficiency in Running**
   a. Forty-yard dash. Average speed—6.8 seconds.
   b. Fifty-yard dash. Average speed—8.0 seconds.
   c. Sixty-yard dash. Average speed—8.2 seconds.
   The crouch start is recommended for these dashes.
   d. Sixty-yard low hurdle (24 inches). Average speed—11.0 seconds.
   e. Shuttle relay race, as described in Chapter 7, page 181.
   f. Potato race. This may be an individual competitive activity or a relay race.

2. **Activities That Develop Proficiency in Jumping**
   a. Stand, hop, step, and jump. Average distance—12 feet.
   b. Stand and broad jump. Average distance—5 feet for boys, 4 feet for girls.
   c. Running broad jump. Average distance—10 feet for boys, 7 feet for girls.
   d. High jump. Average height—3 feet for boys, 2 feet for girls.
3. **Activities That Develop Proficiency in Throwing**
   a. Chest-pass relay (see diagram). One basketball is required for each team of ten.

10	9	8	7	6	5	4	3	2			1	
X	X	X	X	X	X	X	X	X	←	→	X	Leader
X	X	X	X	X	X	X	X	X	12 feet		2	

   Procedure is the same as for all relays.
   b. Forward-pass relay (see page 200). One football is required for each team of ten.
   c. Softball throw. Average distance—90 feet for boys, 70 feet for girls.
   d. Basketball throw. Average distance—60 feet for boys, 40 feet for girls.

The fundamental techniques described in Chapter 3 should be used as guides in attaining correct form for these activities. No track and field events should be permitted on playgrounds that are not suited for this type of activity. They must be omitted from the program unless there is, as there should be, an area where they can be practiced safely. These skills should never be over-emphasized.

SUMMARY

The period of preadolescent growth that begins when children are nine or ten reaches its peak when they are eleven or twelve. Maturity levels, rather than age levels, should therefore continue to be the guide which determines activities for eleven- and twelve-year-olds. Because maturity is an individual matter, individuality is the keynote of this age group.

To meet the needs of these children, this chapter describes some physical education activities that appeal to all the various types within the group and others that satisfy their desire and need to act as individuals as well as a group.

The chapter points out that these children are ready for games of increased organization. It emphasizes the need for helping them develop the ability to evaluate their own achievements and appreciate the achievements of classmates. It suggests activities that unite a heterogeneous group of individuals into a cooperative group, in which each member is group-conscious and eager to have fun as part of the group and, at the same time, able to retain his own individuality.

This chapter reiterates the philosophy of all preceding chapters, which cite enjoyment as the final criterion in evaluating an activity. When an activity or unit has been completed, the true test of its success can be summed up in the expression "Wasn't that fun!"

QUESTIONS AND TOPICS FOR DISCUSSION

1. What specific characteristics that first appear at this age level should be utilized as guides in planning the program of physical education?

2. In what ways may pupil leadership be used to fullest advantage with eleven- and twelve-year-old children?

3. What types of rhythmic activity are best suited for children of this age level?

4. What are the values of track and field activities for eleven- and twelve-year-old children?

5. At this age level, which areas of physical education are best taught (a) coeducationally and (b) to boys and girls separately?

SUGGESTED ACTIVITY UNIT

Plan a unit on the westward movement. The core may be physical education. Because the hardships of the pioneers are often emphasized in the study of the westward movement, it would be interesting to study these early Americans from the standpoint of the fun they had in their few hours of leisure. Weave around this core important factors learned about the socioeconomic status of our forebears.

ADDITIONAL QUESTIONS AND PROBLEMS FOR DISCUSSION—PART TWO

1. How can physical education serve as a core for a unit of instruction?

2. Describe ways in which physical education can supplement a unit.

3. How does a well-planned program of physical education help children develop socially?

4. What have you learned about the correlation between aspects of physical growth and social growth at any given age?

5. In what ways does physical education help teachers discover strengths and weaknesses in children?

6. Discuss differences between *age level* and *maturity level.*

7. When should a teacher be guided by the maturity level of the child more than by the age level?

8. Which physical education activities can be valuable and enjoyable for more than one age group?

9. How do the physical activities for each age group meet the demands for the respective group?

10. Describe a well-balanced program of physical education for the nine- and ten-year-old group.

11. List materials needed to carry on a satisfactory program of physical education for eleven- and twelve-year-olds.

12. Suggest ways and means of developing a satisfactory program of physical education in a school where materials, equipment, and space are at a premium.

SUGGESTED SOURCES OF PHONOGRAPH RECORDS— PART TWO

Primary Music-Rhythms
    Audio Education, Inc.
    New York

Honor Your Partner Records
    Square Dance Associates
    Freeport, N. Y.

Bowmar Records
  Bowmar Company
  Los Angeles, Calif.

Burns and Wheeler Records
  Burns Record Company
  Stratford, Conn.

Creative Rhythms Records
  Whitney's
  San Francisco, Calif.

Childhood Rhythms
  Ruth Evans
  Springfield, Mass.

Decca Records
  The Decca Record Company
  New York

Folk Dancer Records
  The Folk Dancer
  Flushing, N. Y.

Folkraft Records
  Folkraft Records
  Newark, N. J.

Imperial Records
  Imperial Records
  Hollywood, Calif.

MacGregor Records
  MacGregor Records
  Hollywood, Calif.

Methodist Records
  Methodist Publishing
  House
  Nashville, Tenn.

Victor Records
  RCA Victor Record Company
  Camden, N. J.

Windsor Records
  Windsor Records
  Temple City, Calif.

Young People's Records
  Young People's Records
  New York

SUGGESTED REFERENCES—PART TWO

BOOKS

Andrews, G., *Creative Rhythmic Movement for Children.* Englewood Cliffs, N. J.: Prentice-Hall, Inc., 1954.

Bancroft, J., *Games for Home, School, Playground, Gymnasium.* New York: The Macmillan Company, 1931.

Burchenal, E., *Dances of the People.* New York: G. Schirmer, Inc., 1934.

———, *Folk Dances and Singing Games.* New York: G. Schirmer, Inc., 1938.

Cotteral, B., and D. Cotteral, *The Teaching of Stunts and Tumbling.* New York: A. S. Barnes and Company, 1936.

Davis, E., and J. Lawther, *Successful Teaching in Physical Education.* 2d ed., Englewood Cliffs, N. J.: Prentice-Hall, Inc., 1948.

Dexter, Van Hagen, Williams, *Physical Education in Elementary Schools.* Sacramento, Calif.: California State Department of Eduation, 1951.

Duggan, Ann, et al., *Folk Dance Library.* New York: A. S. Barnes and Company, 1948.

Durlacher, E., *Honor Your Partner.* New York: The Devin-Adair Company, 1949.

Evans, R., and E. Battis, *Childhood Rhythms.* New York: Chartwell House, Inc., 1954.

Evans, R., and Leo Gans, *Supervision of Physical Education.* New York: McGraw-Hill Book Company, Inc., 1950.

Fielder, Grace, *The Rhythmic Program for Elementary Schools.* St. Louis: The C. V. Mosby Company, 1952.

Fischer, H., and D. Shawbold, *Individual and Group Stunts.* Minneapolis: Burgess Publishing Company, 1950.

Ford, Mr. & Mrs. Henry, *Good Morning.* Dearborn, Mich.: Dearborn Publishing Company, 1946.

Fraser, E., J. Bransford, and M. Hastings, *The Child and Physical Education.* Englewood Cliffs, N. J.: Prentice-Hall, Inc., 1956.

Geri, F. H. *Games and Rhythms for Children: Primary Grades.* Englewood Cliffs, N. J.: Prentice-Hall, Inc., 1955.

Hunt, P., and C. Underwood, *Calico Rounds.* New York: Harper & Brothers, 1955.

Irwin, Leslie, *The Physical Education Program.* St. Louis: The C. V. Mosby Company, 1944.

Kraus, Richard, *Square Dancing.* New York: A. S. Barnes and Company, 1951.

La Salle, Dorothy, *Rhythms and Dances for Elementary School.* New York: A. S. Barnes and Company, 1926.

Mason, B. S., and E. D. Mitchell, *Party Games for All.* New York: Barnes & Noble, Inc., 1945.

Murray, R., *Dance in Elementary Education.* New York: Harper & Brothers, 1953.

O'Keefe, P., and H. Fahey, *Physical Education in Elementary Schools.* St. Louis: The C. V. Mosby Company, 1949.

Pearl, N. H., and H. E. Brown, *Health by Stunts.* New York: The Macmillan Company, 1926.

Price, M. K., *The Source Book of Play-party Games.* Minneapolis: Burgess Company, 1949.

Rogers, M., *A Handbook of Stunts.* New York: The Macmillan Company, 1940.

Rohrbough, L., *The Handy Play-party Book*. Delaware, Ohio: Co-operative Recreation Service, 1940.

Ryan, G. L., *Dances of Our Pioneers*. New York: A. S. Barnes and Company, 1939.

Sheehy, E. D., *There's Music in Children*. New York: Henry Holt and Company, Inc., 1949.

Sehon, E. L., M. H. Anderson, W. W. Hodgins, and G. R. Van Fossen, *Physical Education Methods for Elementary Schools*. Philadelphia: W. B. Saunders Company, 1953.

Stuart, F., and J. Ludlam, *Rhythmic Activities: Series I and II (cards)*. Minneapolis: Burgess Publishing Company.

Troester, C. A., Jr., *Everyday Games for Children*. Dansville, N. Y.: F. A. Owen Publishing Company, 1950.

Waterman, E. *A, B, C, of Rhythm Training*. Chicago: Clayton Summy Company, 1927.

Whitlock, V., *Come and Caper*. New York: G. Schirmer, Inc., 1932.

Wittich, W. A., and C. F. Schuller, *Audio-Visual Materials*. New York: Harper & Brothers, 1953.

Part Three

Extending the Program:
Special Consideration

9. The Noon Hour

The Noon-hour Problem. Supervision of children during the noon hour is becoming an increasingly serious administrative problem in today's elementary schools, for more and more parents are seeking permission for their children to remain in school the entire day. There seem to be three reasons for this: the distance between home and school, working mothers, and the poor health of the children.

Some children live so far from school that the noon hour does not allow them sufficient time to eat lunch at home. A distance of more than a mile is usually considered too long for children to travel four times a day. Thus children who live at such a distance comprise one group which requires supervision during the noon hour.

A second group includes children from homes where both parents are wage earners. More and more mothers of elementary-school children are seeking employment outside the home, with the result that no one is at home to prepare a midday meal.

A third group which presents a noon-hour problem includes those children whose health might be impaired by walking four times daily between home and school. By remaining in school for lunch, these children may have the advantage of a period of relaxation in the middle of the day.

School systems deal in two ways with the problem of noontime supervision. Some systems schedule a single-session school day. This plan usually entails the provision of cafeteria service, but it eliminates many of the noontime problems. The single-session day allows only a short noon hour, with the schedule so arranged that only a small number of classes go to the cafeteria at one time. There is no crowding and no hurry. Usually each teacher accompanies his class to the dining room and remains with his pupils while they eat lunch together. Each class then participates in a short period of recreation before returning to the classroom for the afternoon.

In school systems with a double-session day the problem of noontime supervision is more serious. The double-session day was planned with the idea that children would travel to their homes for the midday meal. The noon hour in this plan usually ranges from 1 to 1½ hours. Care of the children for a period of this length is a considerable strain upon teachers. The children must be supervised while they are eating and during the longer recreation period. During lunch, both the seating of children and the disposal of waste require careful attention. The fact that some children purchase their lunches in the school cafeteria and others carry theirs from home is an additional problem. During the recreation period, children returning to school after having had lunch at home further complicate the situation. They return in small numbers and naturally wish to join in the play of those already at school. With such a transient group the problems of organization become more difficult. Games once started must be interrupted again and again to admit new players.

With all its problems, however, the noon hour offers an excellent opportunity for educational enrichment. Many children learn to eat more adequate lunches through participation in a well-conducted noon-hour program. Many learn to play more easily with other children.

The reason for this detailed discussion of noon-hour problems is that (1) in an ever-increasing number of elementary schools, both classroom teachers and physical education teachers are assigned the responsibility for this part of the school program and (2) the use of many activities included in well-developed programs of physical education is essential to a successful noon-hour program.

Preparation for the Noon Hour. Children require careful preparation for participation in the elementary-school noon-hour program. Immediate preparation is essential—children require constant reminding about the importance of taking care of toilet needs, washing hands, and attending to general grooming. Long-term preparation, though, is equally important and it may easily develop into purposeful experiences for children if it is made a real part of the school program. Whether or not classroom teachers are called upon actually to supervise children during the noon hour, they share responsibility for planning desirable activities for the noon hour and for preparing children to participate.

Preparation for the noon hour really begins with helping children develop favorable attitudes toward participation in the noon-hour program. Children need to learn that the school lunch service is a privilege granted only to good citizens. A review of the fundamentals of approved table manners provides an excellent classroom activity in health education, as well as important background material for the noon-hour program. Discussions, dramatizations, and reports from children form an essential part of this review. Learning the fundamentals of nutrition proves to be of great value, also. Understanding what constitutes a balanced meal and recognizing the importance of the proper diet contribute to the education of children.

Eating Lunch. Classroom teachers or other personnel who remain with children while they eat their noontime lunch at school bear responsibility for the good conduct of this part of the school program. Orderly seating, the practice of good table manners, and desirable social behavior at the table all contribute to the general success of the program. Children need to know their places at the table, or at least the tables where they are supposed to sit. If the tables are small (seating four), children, especially younger children, should be assigned regular and fairly permanent places. If the tables are large, the children may be assigned to tables and permitted to take seats depending upon the order of their arrival at the table.

Children should be encouraged to eat everything served to them and to leave no food on their plates. Second servings are popular; they are also economical, if first servings are moderately sized. Children, especially the younger group, react favorably to plates not overloaded with food.

Conversation should be carried on among children at each table, but there should be no shouting from table to table. It has been found that appointing children to act as host and hostess at each table helps to moderate lunchroom noise. They take responsibility for leading the conversation at table and for directing the clearing of the table when the meal is over.

Children should be taught and required to practice the correct use of napkin, knife, fork, and spoon. The proper use of drinking straws is an important, though sometimes difficult, skill for children to learn. A child who finds it unpleasant to drink milk from a bottle should be permitted to use a cup or a glass, for if such permission is not granted, the child may refuse to drink milk at all.

The lunch period should be a pleasant time. Children should not feel "held down," but they should not expect to behave in a disorderly manner. Each child should be responsible for carrying his own dishes and tray to the designated place for disposal and for doing his share toward keeping the dining room in good order.

Relaxation after Lunch. Teachers or other adults in charge of the noontime period should require children to remain at the table for a reasonable length of time. Eating should be unhurried; 20 minutes seems an adequate time for children to be seated and to eat the type of meal served in most school lunchrooms. No child should rush from the lunch table to active play. To avoid this, it is desirable to provide a short period of relaxation in which children may listen to a story, to music, or to a well-selected radio or television program. Sometimes it is a good practice to have them just sit quietly in relaxed positions for a while before the active-play program begins.

Active Recreation at Noon. The last part of the noon hour is usually a period of active recreation. During this period the same general standards of organization and behavior should prevail as do during any other part of the school day. Sometimes it is well to organize children into definite teams and groups for participation in highly organized activity; other times it may be better to permit them free selection of activity, individual or group. Many activities learned during other parts of the school program may be enjoyed during the noon-hour recreation period; however, many of the activities that children enjoy most do not appear at all in the school program. Either type of activity may be of great value at this time.

On pleasant days, children enjoy playing many varieties of active outdoor games. Circle games, team games, and small-group games are equally popular. Indoors, children enjoy all sorts of playroom activities. Relay races, rhythms, singing games, folk dances, square dances—all appeal strongly to most children. A list of recommended activities appears at the end of this chapter.

Who Should Supervise the Noon Hour? In many elementary schools, classroom teachers supervise the noon-hour program; in others, supervision is assigned to physical education teachers. Whichever plan is followed, children should never feel that they are responsible for teachers having to assume added duties. No child should be made to feel guilty about something over which he has no control. Noontime supervision, ideally, should be a regular part of some teachers' work and not an additional responsibility.

SUGGESTED ACTIVITIES FOR NOONTIME RECREATION

Indoor Activities—Table Games

Checkers	Flinch
Dominoes	Lotto
Chinese Checkers	Jackstraws
Parchesi	Anagrams
Card games	Tiddlywinks
Old Maid	Jigsaw puzzles
Authors	

Indoor Games—for the Playroom

Shuffleboard	Ringtoss
Bowling	Rubber horseshoes

Indoor Activities—Rhythmics

Fundamental rhythms	Play-party games
Interpretive rhythms	Folk dances
Singing games	Square dances

Indoor Activities—for the Auditorium

Musical programs	Talent shows
Listening to recordings	Radio programs
Community singing	Television programs

Outdoor Programs—for Younger Children

Play on apparatus
  Swings
  Slides
  Jungle-gyms
  Ladders

Group games
  For large groups
  For small groups
  Free play

Outdoor Programs—for Older Children

Group games
  For large groups
  For small groups
Team games
  Volleyball

Softball
Soccer baseball
Line soccer
Basketball (skills)

SUMMARY

Supervision of children during the noon hour is a serious elementary-school problem. An increasingly large number of parents desire and expect their children to remain in school for the entire day. The reasons for this may be (1) the distance between the home and the school, (2) the fact that both parents work outside the home, or (3) the health needs of the children.

Some school systems minimize the need for noon-hour supervision by shortening the midday recess or by making the school day a single session. Other school systems set up a highly organized noon-hour program which comprises the lunch period and an organized program of recreation.

Noontime supervision, in order to function effectively, should cover (1) preparation for the noon hour, (2) the lunch period, and (3) relaxation and recreation.

QUESTIONS AND PROBLEMS FOR DISCUSSION

1. Why is the supervision of elementary-school children during the noon hour an increasingly serious problem?

2. Who should be responsible for noontime supervision?

3. Would the adoption of a single-session day make the problem less difficult?

4. What is involved in preparing children for participation in the noontime program?

5. What are the essentials of good organization and supervision for the period when children are eating lunch?

6. Why is it important for children to relax after eating, before taking part in active play?

7. What types of recreational activity are suitable for the noon hour?

SUGGESTED PROBLEM

You are a supervisor of the noon-hour program in an elementary school. You have thirty children to supervise from 11:45 to 12:45. Plan programs that will include preparation, eating, relaxing, and activities for the following age groups.

1. Five- and six-year group
2. Seven- and eight-year group
3. Nine- and ten-year group
4. Eleven- and twelve-year group

If your group varied in age from five to twelve years, how would this fact alter your plans?

10. Rainy Days

W**hat Teachers Say.** Rainy days test the patience and endurance of even the best teachers. The following statements, sometimes uttered in seeming despair, express a common sentiment:

"If I live through today, I can stand anything."

"My children seem possessed today. I can't do anything with them."

"I'm worn out, and it's only noontime."

"Rainy days try my patience."

Such remarks may often be overheard in the teachers' room of an elementary school. Probably no group of workers notices more keenly than teachers of young children the effect weather has upon human behavior. Anyone associated with elementary-school teachers accustoms himself to their comments about the children's reactions to various weather conditions and changes in climate.

The Influence of Weather on Human Behavior. It is generally believed, despite little scientific evidence, that weather influences the way a person feels and behaves. Much has been said about the problem. Some opinions are undoubtedly based upon superstition, although numerous convictions have grown out of personal experience and a few of them do merit examination. Many persons, including some scientists, believe that people and animals react in certain ways to approaching storms. People and animals, they say, become irritable and restless before a storm. Animals sometimes act surly and become unruly. Human beings may become absent-minded. It is even said that efficiency decreases when the barometer falls.

Many persons believe that people work best in pleasant weather, but this hypothesis has little scientific foundation. Bright days bring inspiration, perhaps, but not always inspiration for

234

work. Spring fever may or may not be imaginary. The first warm days of spring are enjoyable, but vitality may be lower at this season. Human bodies must work hard to adjust themselves to sharp seasonal rises in temperature by throwing off the extra body heat they need in winter.

The fact remains that people often refer to weather and climate in connection with the way they feel and the things they do. We constantly hear such expressions as:

"A face as black as a thunder cloud."
"What a blue day this is."
"This rain is soft and peaceful."
"Tonight is a good night for sleeping."
"It's cool today; now I can work."

Effect of Weather on Children in School. Teachers of elementary-school children present evidence to support the view that young people change their behavior patterns as the weather changes. What about these changes? Some teachers contend that young children become lethargic and stodgy and often shirk their duties on warm, humid days. Most teachers agree that children work well on crisp, cool days. Windy days bring behavior problems, for when the wind blows, children often become restless and uneasy. They grow excitable and irresponsible.

The worst of all weather problems, according to many teachers, is the rainy day. On windy days, on cold days, and on warm days, children may go outdoors for play periods. When it rains, however, whether or not the school provides adequate indoor play facilities, children and teachers must remain indoors. And an indoor play period on a rainy day is a strain on the nerves of young and old alike.

Weather Affects Teachers, Too. Adults react to warm, humid, windy, and rainy days just as definitely as children do. Thus teachers, as well as children, find the rainy day a test of good behavior and self-control. The teacher, however, faces this problem as an adult, while the members of the class are immature. It is the responsibility of the teacher to exercise the needed self-control, to remain on even keel, and to recognize the fact that the behavior of children may be influenced both by weather and by teacher example.

Teachers who carefully plan a rainy-day recreation program, providing for activities which arouse the imagination and challenge the originality of pupils, usually find that good discipline and wholesome relationships are quite easily established. But irritable teachers who snap at children and teachers who fail to make allowance for the effect of weather on young people sometimes find themselves in difficult positions. Children in such classes often become disorderly and uncooperative, and their teachers may well complain of being exhausted at the end of the school day.

How to Plan for Rainy Days. What types of activity are best suited to the rainy-day recreation program? The type of activity depends somewhat upon the facilities at hand and the ability of the teacher to make full use of them. It also depends upon the degree of formality which ordinarily exists in the classroom. Imaginative, resourceful teachers plan well in advance for rainy-day recreation, fortifying themselves with interesting activities for their children on bad days. In schools with adequate indoor playroom facilities, the problem is serious enough, but it is far more difficult in schools where recreational and physical education activities must be conducted in the classrooms.

One of the dangers to be considered in planning rainy-day recreational programs is the possibility of overstimulating the children. On rainy days children are likely to participate so vigorously in play activities that they become overexcited and unfit to return to the academic program. Children fatigued both physically and nervously by active play can accomplish little academically.

The recreation period should provide a means of release from tension caused by periods of intensive and demanding study. It should also provide opportunity for children to learn and practice challenging play skills. But school recreation should not interfere with the general school program. Recreation should be a part of, rather than in competition with, the whole curriculum.

In an elementary school equipped with one or more playrooms, the program of recreation may be varied to suit the interests of individual children. The advantages of varied programs are many and great.

A well-planned, varied program of school recreation includes more than a few simple games. Where facilities permit, all the following activities may be utilized. Play-party games involving simple skills, and dance steps which may be learned quickly and enjoyed again and again are popular with children. Typical of these play-party games are Skip to My Lou, the Broom Dance, and the fun dances.

Social dancing is also popular with children as a rainy-day activity. Children enjoy hopping and whirling about to the lively music of a brisk polka. Gay waltzes, too, appeal to young people. Social dancing proves especially successful as a rainy-day recreational activity if teachers participate along with the children. Changing partners in a Paul Jones or some friendly method of tagging makes social dancing more fun for boys and girls of elementary-school age. Small-group games, such as shuffleboard and ringtoss, are also excellent media of entertainment that require comparatively little skill.

Carefully organized, well-conducted talent shows are another interesting diversion. This type of activity, however, has sometimes been used to excess. Children who sing well, play musical instruments, have unusual skill in dancing, or recite easily are welcomed as entertainers by their classmates. But the exploitation of children whose talent is not marked or whose selection of material is not in good taste should not be encouraged. Teachers need to be constantly on guard against this sort of thing.

Some schools lack playrooms, and some schools do not have corridors wide enough for recreational use. Schools with no play space other than classrooms present a serious problem. Teachers in buildings of this type must exercise unusual organizing ability and great imaginative power in planning for rainy-day recreation. The strain on these teachers is great. The situation, however, presents a challenge. Utilizing a classroom as a recreation center means improvising all sorts of original activities which can be conducted in the small space available. Such activities are listed and described at the end of this chapter.

Criteria for the Selection of Rainy-day Activities. Criteria for the selection of rainy-day recreational activities are based on acceptable principles of education. The activities should (1) interest the children, (2) provide opportunity for the development of skills, however simple they may be, (3) include at least some physical activity, (4) be adaptable to limited classroom space, and (5) present no safety hazards. Games played in circles around the room and games including simple tricks or stunts provide good material for these programs. The organization of the class for such activities should be informal but orderly. Children should learn how to enjoy themselves without creating any disorder or confusion.

SUGGESTED RAINY-DAY ACTIVITIES

Classroom Activities
A. Zogging
   1. *Equipment*
      None
   2. *Number of Players*
      Two in each group
   3. *Directions*
      Players sit facing each other. The game consists of the use of several gestures, each of which has a meaning. The gestures are (a) a hand made into a fist to represent a rock, (b) a hand extended flat, with the palm up, to represent a piece of paper, (c) a hand extended, with the first two fingers separated, to represent a pair of scissors. The meanings attached to the gestures are (a) a rock dulls scissors, (b) paper wraps up a rock, (c) scissors cut paper.

      The players agree upon a starting signal; when it is given, they both slap the right fist in the palm of the left hand, and each extends his hand, using whichever of the gestures he wishes.

      A point is scored each time a player "dulls scissors with a rock," "cuts paper with scissors," or "wraps up a rock with paper." If one player extends his hand as a rock and the other extends his as scissors, the second player receives a point. The game has a given time limit. Players may change partners after each time period to make competition more interesting.

B. Malaga Grapes

  1. *Equipment*
    A cane or a baton

  2. *Number of Players*
    Any number

  3. *Directions*
    Children sit in their chairs while one at a time comes to the front of the room to take a turn at repeating, *exactly* as the leader said it, the jingle "Malaga grapes, malaga grapes, the best we have in the market." The leader starts the game by reciting the jingle while beating time with the cane. As he recites it he does something special which he tries to keep the player from noticing but which the player must repeat when he recites. The catch may be that the leader unobtrusively clears his throat at some point in reciting the jingle. Another catch might be that he changes his cane from one hand to the other or performs some other simple movement.

C. Scissors Crossed and Uncrossed

  1. *Equipment*
    A pair of scissors

  2. *Number of Players*
    Any number

  3. *Directions*
    Children sit in an informal group and pass a pair of scissors from one to the other around the group. As each child passes the scissors to the next player, he says, "I take the scissors crossed; I pass them on uncrossed." As each child takes the scissors, they are open (closed). As each child passes the scissors on to the next child, they are uncrossed (crossed). The trick is that when the word "crossed" is said, the knees should be crossed; when the word "uncrossed" is said, the knees should be uncrossed. Each child should try to cross and uncross his knees so that the others will not notice. The scissors go round and round the group. Each child who does the trick correctly scores 1 point. The game is played for a limited time or until all the children know the trick.

D. Circle Passes
1. *Equipment*
   Several small objects to be passed
2. *Number of Players*
   Any number
3. *Directions*
   The children stand in a large circle, all facing the center. The captain is given two small objects. He starts the first of these around the circle, and each child receives it and passes it to the next. As soon as one object is on the way, the captain starts the second one. The idea is to see whether the second object will overtake the first.

E. Neighbor, Neighbor
1. *Equipment*
   None
2. *Number of Players*
   Any number
3. *Directions*
   Children sit side by side in a circle. One child stoops low and sits on his haunches; in this position he hops around the circle and stops in front of a child, to whom he says, "Neighbor, neighbor, how art thou?" The other child answers, "Pretty well, I thank thee now." The first child then says, "How's the neighbor next to thee?" The second child answers, "I don't know, but I'll go see." This child then changes places with the first child and hops around the circle, stopping in front of the child who was his next neighbor. The game continues as long as interest holds.

F. Lion Hunt
1. *Equipment*
   None
2. *Number of Players*
   Any number
3. *Directions*
   Children are seated in a group. The teacher or leader stands facing the group. The leader starts to recite the following story. The children repeat each statement made by the leader and imitate her motions.

"Let's go on a lion hunt." Children repeat.

"Come on." Starting with hands on their knees, children slap their knees with alternate hands to simulate walking.

"Wonder where the lions are." They continue the same motion.

"Here's a hill; let's go up." Lifting their hands higher, they slap more slowly.

"Here's the top; let's go down." They slap faster, as though running.

"Here's a brook; let's jump it." They slap fast and end with a big slap.

"It's dark here." They slap slowly.

"I'm scared." They slap slowly.

"See any lions?" Hands above their eyes, they look left and right.

"There's one." No motion.

"Let's go home." They reverse all the motions from the beginning.

G. Musical Chairs

1. *Equipment*

Chairs for all but one player

2. *Number of Players*

As many as space will accommodate

3. *Directions*

As the music starts, the children start marching around the chairs. When the music stops, all try to secure chairs. The child without a chair is eliminated from the game. One chair is taken away, and the game is repeated. Game continues until there is but one chair left and two children to play.

If this game is played in a classroom with permanently fixed furniture, a book may be placed on each chair that would ordinarily be taken away.

H. Seven Chairs

1. *Equipment*

Seven chairs arranged in a row in the front of the room

2. *Number of Players*
   Any number

3. *Directions*
   Three boys and three girls are selected to sit on chairs, as in Figure 10–1. The center chair is left unoccupied. One child is selected to direct the game. He must move the girls to the boys' chairs and the boys to the girls' chairs. He must move the players one at a time. Each change must be either a move to the chair next to the one the player now occupies or a jump over *one* chair. Boys and girls must move in opposite directions. Each of their moves is counted aloud by the children who are observing. When the child directing the moves reaches an impasse, he must give up his place to another, who starts from the beginning. The child who accomplishes the entire change with the fewest moves wins the game.

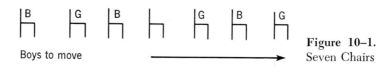

Boys to move

Girls' direction for moving

Figure 10–1.
Seven Chairs

I. Human Ticktacktoe

1. *Equipment*
   Nine chairs arranged three in a row

2. *Number of Players*
   Any number of observers, two directors

3. *Directions*
   Boys and girls form opposing teams. One boy and one girl are selected to direct the game. First the girl, then the boy, seats a member of his team according to the rules of the pencil-and-paper version of ticktacktoe. A win scores 1 point. The number of games to be played should be agreed upon before play is started.

J. Bowling in the Aisles

1. *Equipment*
   Several sets of bowling pins. (Class-made pins serve nicely.

These may be regular blackboard erasers or cardboard cylinders such as come in rolls of paper towels). Three balls for each set of pins.

2. *Number of Players*

   Any number, divided into teams of even size

3. *Directions*

   With each aisle in the classroom serving as a bowling alley, the pins are set up at the front of the room, with 8 inches between pins and between the rows of pins. A starting line is drawn across each aisle at the back of the room. Each child takes his turn at bowling, scoring the game as much like regular bowling as possible.

K. **Human Checkers**

1. *Equipment*

   A classroom with permanently fixed furniture

2. *Number of Players*

   Any number, boys playing against girls

3. *Directions*

   a. Boys go to one side of room, girls to other.

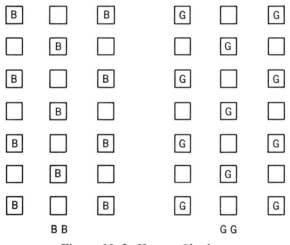

Figure 10–2. Human Checkers

   b. Two boys are selected to direct the boys, two girls to direct the girls.

   c. Half the room should be used for boys, and half for

girls. Children should be seated according to Figure 10–2, with children sitting in every other seat, as the squares are arranged on a checkerboard. Extra players observe.

d. The two boys and the two girls who are to direct their teams move their players around as they would checkers on a checkerboard. The rules are the same as for checkers.

Note: An excellent way to introduce this game is to have a demonstration game of regular checkers played, so that all the children will learn the rules.

Additional Activities

Playroom Activities	*Play-party Games*
Shuffleboard	Jolly Is the Miller
Ball bouncing	A-hunting We Will Go
Rope jumping	Push the Business On
Jackstones	The Muffin Man
Deck tennis	O Susannah
	Pop Goes the Weasel

SUMMARY

There is a strong opinion that weather influences human behavior. Although there is little scientific evidence to prove this point, teachers in elementary schools generally agree that there should be carefully planned physical education on rainy days.

On rainy days especially, overstimulation of the children must be avoided. Activities that challenge the imagination often prove more successful than those of a more vigorous nature. Activities with a flavor of social recreation are very acceptable. Activities which are a little unusual make the rainy-day physical education period a pleasure.

Rainy-day activities should (1) be interesting to children, (2) provide a challenge in respect to skill development, even though the skills may be simple, (3) include some physical activity, (4) be adaptable to classroom space, and (5) present no safety hazards.

QUESTIONS AND TOPICS FOR DISCUSSION

1. Does weather influence human behavior? If so, how?
2. How should a teacher of elementary-school children plan for rainy-day programs of physical education?
3. What are some criteria for the selection of rainy-day activities?

SUGGESTED ACTIVITY UNIT

Develop a unit of study on the ways in which weather affects the play activities of children in different regions of our country. This study should include research about several climatic regions, seasonal changes, and the effect these changes have on play activities. A reservoir of seasonal games, dances, stunts, and rhythmic activities may be prepared.

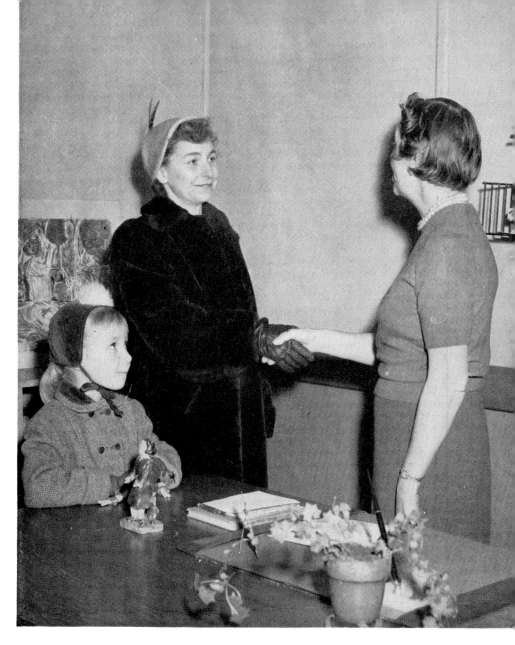

11. Community Relations through Special Programs

A School Is a Part of the Community. A school is not a desert island located within the community but isolated from it. A school is an agency supported by and belonging to the community. What goes on within a school is the business of the citizens whose taxes provide financial support for public education. Citizens of the community are represented in the school organization by those of their group who are elected or appointed to serve on the board of education; however, school community relations should not be limited to this. The school should take responsibility for acquainting the public with philosophy, policies, and programs.

Each area of the educational program has specific points of interest for persons outside the school organization. Some citizens take great interest in the program of musical education. To these people the progress made by a school band, orchestra, or choral group means important educational achievement. Other citizens are very much interested in athletics. To them a winning team means a successful and satisfactory program of education. Still other patrons of public schools show particular interest in the so-called fundamental subjects of the curriculum. The level of achievement indicated by student scores on standard reading and mathematics tests provides these people with a means of evaluating the schools in the community. Because of the diverse interests of citizens in the community, public schools should make every effort to inform the public of the progress being made in all phases of education.

ESTABLISHING COMMUNITY RELATIONS

School systems and individual schools utilize various methods of keeping the public informed of their policies and progress. News-

papers, radio, and television are generally accepted as fundamental media for good public relations. Through these channels all
citizens in the community may be informed of the activities of
any community organization. Parent-teacher association meetings
provide another efficient means of communicating with patrons of
public education. Speeches prepared and delivered by faculty
members, discussions conducted by parent-teacher groups and
participated in by both parents and teachers, and programs which
demonstrate the school activities of the children—all contribute to
the value of such meetings. Participation of faculty members and
students in the meetings of other groups in the community, such
as service clubs, civic organizations, church groups, and fraternal
organizations, can be mutually profitable to all. Such participation
is welcomed by the groups involved and serves as an excellent
means of establishing friendly community relations. Most citizens, individually and in groups, are eager to learn about the programs of education being carried on in local schools.

The Satisfied Customer. The schools have within their own
walls the most effective ambassadors of good will. These are the
children who are attending school, enjoying profitable experiences, recognizing their own individual strengths and weaknesses,
accepting responsibilities as young citizens, and attaining success
in their school venture.

All parents want assurance that their child is getting ahead in
school, that their son or daughter is learning and experiencing
things that contribute to wholesome development. They gain some
measure of this assurance when the child tells of his thrilling experiences in physical education and of the satisfaction derived
from physical education activities.

The parents of the second-grade children of one city school
became very enthusiastic about the educational advantages provided at "their children's school." This enthusiasm was not due to
a careful study of the school's program but, rather, to the results
of the program related by the children themselves. These children
went home with such remarks as, "Guess what we did today! We
learned to waltz," or "I can't wait until tomorrow! We're going
to learn a new game," or "You should see Johnny now! He can
run as fast as I can." Each parent-teacher conference was prefaced

by a story, related to the teacher by the parent, about the school's contribution to the happiness and educational progress of that parent's child. At parent-teacher association meetings the parents were generous in their praise of the school and happy with their children's part in the school program. Thus, children themselves may represent the best type of community relations.

School Visits. Encouraging parents to visit schools frequently; making each visit pleasant, friendly, and worthwhile; and helping parents, through their visits, to become acquainted with ordinary school routine—all provide opportunities for parents and school personnel to clarify the problems, successes, and failures of the children. The parents of the children described in the preceding paragraph frequently visited the classroom. One mother who came to school with her preschool child said, "I just had to come today. Amy wanted Baby Brother to see how well the children can dance." Little brothers and sisters just *had* to see every new achievement of these children, who were confident that their teacher would welcome the little visitors and their mothers.

In addition to encouraging family visits, this teacher invites parents actually to participate in some of the musical and rhythmic activities of the group. One mother enjoyed periodic dance fests with the children. She played the violin for them as they square-danced. Another mother helped a group learn to play ukuleles to accompany their singing activities. Whenever a child made some such comment as, "My father can play the accordion," that parent was invited to share his ability with his child's classmates. Most parents who were given this opportunity were eager to contribute to the learning experiences of their children.

One parent was told by the teacher that his child was exceptionally rhythmic and that he added to class enjoyment of rhythms by beating time on his desk. At Christmas the child received a set of miniature drums, which the parent transported to school and left there for the remainder of the school year; moreover, the parent made it clear to the teacher that all the children should be given an opportunity to experiment with the drums. Needless to say, interest in rhythmic activities was high. Other miniature instruments made their appearance, and parents, relatives, and friends often came to the practice sessions.

In a school where parents and friends are frequent visitors, the content of the curriculum becomes familiar to the community members, problems are discussed as they arise, and misunderstandings do not grow into controversial issues.

School Demonstrations. Some parts of the school program lend themselves readily to discussion or demonstration; other parts of the program are more difficult to clarify for those not directly concerned with education. Physical education provides many possibilities for demonstration. The remainder of this chapter deals with suggestions for special physical education activities which may prove valuable to programs designed to promote community and public relations.

PROGRAM DEMONSTRATIONS

The parents of elementary-school children usually show great interest in their children's ability to perform physical activity skills. An excellent way to make it possible for parents to observe their children's performance is to conduct demonstrations of physical education activities in which all children participate. When planning such a demonstration, teachers should try to use the regular facilities rather than to transfer the program to an unfamiliar setting. For example, activities which are regularly conducted in a playroom are not demonstrated to good advantage on an auditorium stage. Activities which require outdoor space cannot be satisfactorily carried on in a gymnasium or playroom, where space is limited.

Standards of performance for a program demonstration should, naturally, be high, but only as high as the whole group can attain. If the demonstration is to be successful, all students must participate, not just a selected group of superior performers. Artificial standards are not a fair indication of average student ability and are undesirable for a program demonstration.

Elementary-school physical education activities lend themselves easily to a program demonstration which enables spectators to see the many types of activity that comprise the physical education program and also to get an idea of the progression from one age level to another within a specific activity. Both factors are important and prove to be of great interest to observers.

Group Activities for Program Demonstration

The activities listed below are typical of those included in daily programs of physical education for elementary-school children. These activities require the development of specific neuromuscular skills, which are essential to participation in vigorous physical activity, and also provide wholesome and enjoyable recreation.

Little or no special preparation is needed to prepare these activities for demonstration purposes. Class standards, if adequate, are perfectly satisfactory for program demonstration. Daily class standards should always represent the achievement that results when every member of the group does his best. Each child should be expected to accomplish as much as he can, and a teacher who knows the individual characteristics of the children sees to it that this happens. Actually, any well-planned and competently conducted class period in physical education could serve as a program demonstration.

Activities for Lower Grades

    Games for large groups
        Busy Bee
        Circle stoop
    Games for small groups
        Wastebasket ball
        Triangle target
    Stunts
        Forward rolls
        Logroll
    Races
        Animal race
        Simple relays
    Fundamental rhythms
        Walking
        Running
        Skipping
        Swaying

Interpretive rhythms
 Animals
 Toys
 Fanciful characters
 Play rhythms
Singing games
 Punchinello
 I Wish I Had a Windmill
Folk dances
 Chimes of Dunkirk
 Bow, Bow, Belinda

Activities for Upper Grades

Games for large groups
 Four All Around
 Streets and Alleys
Games for small groups
 Basketball relay
 Shuffleboard
Stunts
 Forward rolls
 Back rolls
 Head stands
 Simple pyramids
Races
 Shuttle relay
 Over-and-under relay
Fundamental rhythms
 Running
 Skipping
 Sliding
 Folding
Folk dances
 Sicilian Circle
 Little Man in a Fix
Square dances
 First Two Ladies
 Portland Fancy

Dance Festivals

Dance festivals or demonstrations of dance activity represent another suitable type of physical education demonstration. Dances and rhythms lend themselves well to demonstration purposes. Dance movement displays to advantage the achievement of grace and poise, and the group patterns characteristic of many dances readily suggest the social values of this area of physical education. The musical accompaniment adds much to the attractiveness of this type of demonstration.

Dance-demonstration programs may take many forms. The old-time May festival, with a maypole serving as the center of interest, is usually a popular dance program. International dance festivals are delightful. All-American dance festivals are, of course, interesting because of the patriotic flavor. Pan-American dance programs demonstrate the differences between the dance patterns of the United States and those of the Latin-American countries.

Dance-demonstration programs fit easily into larger units. The relation between dancing and social studies makes possible a broad correlation of school activities which clarifies the relation of one area of education to another and permits parents of elementary-school children to see their children's education in its broad sense. Several types of such programs are outlined below.

English May Day Festival. A May Day program may easily be assembled from numerous sources. There are many books containing directions for maypole dances. Characteristic dances for the shepherds and jesters may be original dance patterns composed by children in their physical education classes. Excellent music is available as accompaniment for such dances. The music for Shakespeare's *King Henry the Eighth* is suggested as one possibility. English country dances, for the villagers, are available in many folk-dance books. The order for such a program might be:

Processional—May king and queen, members of the court, villagers, jesters, shepherds
Dance of the villagers—English country dances
Dance of the shepherds—characteristic dance
Dance of the jesters—characteristic dance
The Maypole dance
Recessional

International Dance Festival. The dances for this type of program may easily be introduced through a social studies unit. Also, it is often possible to include in international dance programs dances which children learn at home from their parents, grandparents, and other older members of their families. Children take great pride in teaching their own dances to their friends at school if the correct emphasis is placed by teachers upon the values of national background and folklore. The following dances might be included in such a program.

Dances of Great Britain
    English Ribbon Dance
    Highland Schottische
    Old Welsh Dance
    Irish Lilt
Scandinavian Dances
    Norwegian Mountain Dance
    Swedish Clap Dance
    The Hatter (Danish)
    The Finnish Reel
Dances of the Netherlands
    Dutch Couples
    Chimes of Dunkirk
German Dances
    Little Man in a Fix
    Kinder Polka
European Dances
    Kolo
    Swiss May Dance
    Slovak Dance

American Dance Festival. An American dance program may serve to demonstrate the dance patterns of various periods in American history or may take the form of square-dance programs. Either type is quite acceptable as a means of fostering good community relations. Two programs are suggested below.

Square-dance Program
    Virginia Reel (long set)
    Dive for the Oyster (square set)
    Portland Fancy (changing sets)

Nellie Gray (square singing set)

Money Musk (square set)

American Dance Program

Colonial Days

Minuet

Gavotte

Covered Wagon Days

Virginia Reel

Mountain Reel

Post-Civil War Dances

Badger Gavotte

Lancers

Gay Nineties

Rye Waltz

Trilby Two-step

Modern American Country Dances

Put Your Little Foot

Patty Cake Polka

Play-party Games

Skip to my Lou

Ach, Ja

Pan-American Dance Festival. A Pan-American dance program may include typical dances of North America, South America, and Central America. A suggested list of such dances follows.

Mexican Waltz

La Raspa

Buffalo Boys

Birdie in the Cage

Texas Schottische

Heel-and-toe Polka

Oxford Minuet

Donkey Dance

The preparation of dance programs for demonstration should not entail any appreciable amount of special rehearsing. If the total program of physical education has been planned with the idea that dances may be used for demonstrations, the daily lessons in physical education should represent an ideal learning situation and should provide enough material for a dance program.

Special Demonstrations

For the purpose of acquainting parents and others with the abilities of students or for the purpose of raising money for a worthy cause, the school as a whole may plan and conduct a special type of demonstration program, such as a pageant or musical show. Physical education activities are important to such programs and usually receive strong emphasis.

With no intent to minimize the value of pageants, a word of caution must be expressed. When a pageant is being prepared, it is usually an all-school affair. As those in charge of such a program have a rightful desire to achieve a high standard, rehearsals for the program may take too much time from other phases of physical education and from other school subjects. All too often under these circumstances the program of physical education for many children is limited to preparing their part of the pageant. Teachers should see that a balance is maintained and that rehearsing for the pageant is as enjoyable for children as participating in the various recreational phases of the school's physical education program.

Field Days

A field day program is one excellent way to demonstrate to students and parents the children's ability to run, jump, play games, compete individually and in groups, and maintain self-control under pressure. A field day may also provide one type of wholesome interschool competition for children of elementary-school age. Little has been said in this book about interschool competition because so few schools have built a firm enough foundation in physical education to be ready for this extended type of program. The field day serves well as a transition between the program which is limited to one school and the highly organized interschool program which few educators desire or approve of for elementary-school children.

A field day program should include activities suited to the needs, abilities, interests, and capacities of boys and girls of elementary-school age. Participation should be open to all children, not limited to superior performers. The following is a suggested outline for a field day program:

Field Day Program

  Individual Events

      Thirty-yard dash—boys and girls

      Basketball throw—girls

      Forward pass—boys

  Team Events

      Shuttle relay—boys and girls

      Potato race (modified)—boys and girls

      Cumulative standing broad jump—boys and girls

  Special Events

      Volleyball game—boys and girls

      Soccer-baseball game—boys and girls

Costumes and Properties for Special Programs

In order that a certain amount of glamour be attached to a special program costumes and special properties are often provided. These touches remove the program from the level of daily routine and give it a special significance. Children become enthusiastic about "dressing the part." They enjoy wearing clothes that dramatize the activity in which they are participating.

Interestingly enough, children are just as happy with a suggestion of costuming as with an elaborate outfit. A bright cap or sash, a jacket or an apron worn over children's regular clothing may lend just the touch that is needed to tone up an activity for a demonstration. Children often have excellent ideas concerning costume suggestions, and these should be followed whenever possible.

In the case of more complete costuming, it is desirable for parents and teachers to share the responsibility for selection, planning, and preparation. Parents enjoy having a part in their children's demonstration programs, and teachers, on the other hand, appreciate parents' cooperation.

Whether costuming is complete or suggestive, the cost should be kept to a minimum. Expensive materials and elaborate trimmings are not essential to the success of a school physical education demonstration. The value of a demonstration, or of any special program, lies in the part played by the children, the learning accomplished, and the community relations established.

SUMMARY

Chapter 2 emphasizes the uniqueness of physical education's contribution to wholesome, happy child development. This chapter emphasizes ways in which this uniqueness contributes to the development of wholesome, happy community relations. It shows how daily, anecdotal records furnished parents by their children help to establish the true foundation of an intelligent, understanding, and sympathetic relationship between home and school. It shows how community relations may be further cemented or enhanced through the media of special programs, demonstrations, fiestas, or pageants, but it warns against overrehearsing or overemphasizing special programs at the expense of a balanced program in physical education or other school subjects.

The underlying purpose of this chapter is to reiterate the beliefs upon which the book is based:

1. Children need an atmosphere of wholesome, democratic living in order to prepare themselves for group living in a complex society.

2. Children should be given many opportunities for enrichment of living that improves personal and general welfare.

3. It is the responsibility of school personnel and members of the community in general to provide children with both these requirements. Physical education provides many opportunities for doing so.

4. The ultimate foundation for good school-community relations is, of course, the welfare, progress, and happiness of the children of the community. Thus these children become ambassadors of good will between home and school.

QUESTIONS AND PROBLEMS FOR DISCUSSION

1. Why is it essential for schools to establish community-relations programs?

2. In what ways does physical education lend itself to the community-relations program? Which phases of physical education serve best in this respect?

3. Why are demonstrations of physical education activities of such great value to the community-relations program? What are

some fundamental principles to be observed in planning a physical education demonstration?

SUGGESTED ACTIVITY UNITS

Plan two units designed to promote happy community relations—one which depends on regular classroom activities for this purpose and one which utilizes a school program prepared around a central theme. The theme may be May Day, or it may be one that demonstrates skill progression in physical education from kindergarten through sixth grade.

Appendix

Music for Rhythms and Dances

MUSIC FOR CHAPTER 5

WALKING

RUNNING

SKIPPING

HOPPING

GALLOPING

SWAY AND TWIST

SWING

WALK AND BOW

WALK AND HOP

RUN AND JUMP

UP AND DOWN

ROUND AND ROUND

FAST AND SLOW

DUCKS

CAMELS

HORSES

BIRDS

ELEPHANTS

KANGAROOS

GIANTS

DWARFS

WITCHES

FAIRIES

SWINGS

SEESAWS

TOPS

BICYCLES

ROWBOATS

THE MUFFIN MAN

DID YOU EVER SEE A LASSIE?

TWO LITTLE BLACKBIRDS

PUNCHINELLO

A-HUNTING WE WILL GO

THE MULBERRY BUSH

I WISH I HAD A WINDMILL

THE FARMER IN THE DELL

LOOBY LOO

MUSIC FOR CHAPTER 6

FUNDAMENTAL RHYTHM—WALKING

UP AND DOWN

ROUND AND ROUND

WALK, WALK, HOP, HOP, STOP

RUN, HOP, STOP

LONG STEPS—SHORT STEPS

SWINGING

SUSTAINED MOVEMENT

RUNNING IN PHRASES

THE THREAD FOLLOWS THE NEEDLE

HOW D'YE DO, MY PARTNER

RIG-A-JIG-JIG

JOLLY IS THE MILLER

PUSH THE BUSINESS ON

SEVEN STEPS

A

B

C

BOW, BOW, BELINDA

CHIMES OF DUNKIRK

MUSIC FOR CHAPTER 7

POLKA

WALTZ

TWO-STEP

SCHOTTISCHE

BEANSETTING

Slowly

LITTLE MAN IN A FIX

SELLENGER'S ROUND

A

B

COME, LET US BE JOYFUL

CSEBOGAR

MINUET

IRISH LILT

PUT YOUR LITTLE FOOT

KOLO

O! SUSANNA

WEGGIS

Verse

Chorus

HEEL-AND-TOE POLKA

NELLIE GRAY

FIRST TWO LADIES

NIXIE POLKA

DONKEY DANCE

POP GOES THE WEASEL

MAYPOLE DANCE

MUSIC FOR CHAPTER 8

VIRGINIA REEL

PORTLAND FANCY

RED RIVER VALLEY

SICILIAN CIRCLE

NORWEGIAN MOUNTAIN DANCE

KANAFASKA

CAPTAIN JINKS

TEXAS SCHOTTISCHE

Index